Ignatius Donnelly

The Golden Bottle

The Story of Ephraim Benezet of Kansas

Ignatius Donnelly

The Golden Bottle
The Story of Ephraim Benezet of Kansas

ISBN/EAN: 9783744677752

Printed in Europe, USA, Canada, Australia, Japan

Cover: Foto ©ninafisch / pixelio.de

More available books at **www.hansebooks.com**

PREFACE.

I FEEL that some apology is due to the public for the following book.

I am well aware that it is without that polish and elaboration which should always distinguish literary work. It was hurriedly written, much of it on my knee, in railroad cars, and at country hotels, in the intervals between campaign speeches. It scarcely aspires to be called a *work*. It is what they denominate in England a "*skit*."

It is the outgrowth of the great political struggle now going on, in this year of grace, 1892, in the United States; and it is intended to explain and defend, in the thin disguise of a story, some of the new ideas put forth by the People's Party; and which concern, I sincerely believe, all the peoples of the civilized world. I have a hope that the interest of "THE GOLDEN BOTTLE" may not end with the events which gave it birth.

It is not of so much importance that the author

should glorify himself, by the perfection of his workmanship, as that he should set his readers to *thinking;* and thereby, perhaps, open new gateways to better conditions of life for the multitude. If these ends can be obtained I shall be utterly indifferent to all other considerations and consequences.

I have no doubt the intelligent reader will have sense enough to draw the line where argument ends and romance begins. I would be sorry if any one should be so foolish as to argue that the triumph of the People's Party means a declaration of war against the whole world.

If there is anything in this book which is sensible and reasonable, it will, I trust, be credited to the new political movement; whatever is otherwise can be laid at my door.

And so, with these excuses, and with all its sins and imperfections on its head, I send out "THE GOLDEN BOTTLE," and consign it to the tender mercies of its friends and the serrated teeth of its critics.

I. D.

CONTENTS.

CHAPTER I.
	PAGE
Who I Am, and What I Thought,	9

CHAPTER II.
| What I Saw, | 15 |

CHAPTER III.
| The Golden Nail, | 17 |

CHAPTER IV.
| We Visit Kansas City, | 25 |

CHAPTER V.
| Rich, | 29 |

CHAPTER VI.
| Going Home, | 38 |

CHAPTER VII.
| I Begin Work, | 48 |

CHAPTER VIII.
| The Thunderbolt, | 53 |

CHAPTER IX.
| Doing Business on a Large Scale, | 59 |

CHAPTER X.
| A Millionaire, | 66 |

CONTENTS.

CHAPTER XI.
Sophie, ... 72

CHAPTER XII.
Revenge, ... 78

CHAPTER XIII.
Sophie's Plan, ... 88

CHAPTER XIV.
The Meeting, ... 93

CHAPTER XV.
I Hear from Kansas, ... 108

CHAPTER XVI.
Archibald M. Hayes' Letter, ... 117

CHAPTER XVII.
I Appeal to Congress, ... 121

CHAPTER XVIII.
How Plutocracy Worked, ... 131

CHAPTER XIX.
I Get Mad, ... 148

CHAPTER XX.
The Glad Tidings of Great Joy, ... 152

CHAPTER XXI.
The Financial World, ... 157

CHAPTER XXII.
I Organize the Brotherhood of Justice, . . . 159

CHAPTER XXIII.
I Start a Town and Build a Railroad, . . . 164

CONTENTS.

CHAPTER XXIV.
The Demonetization of Gold, ... 173

CHAPTER XXV.
I Am Elected President, ... 181

CHAPTER XXVI.
A Civil War Probable, ... 185

CHAPTER XXVII.
How the War was Averted, ... 189

CHAPTER XXVIII.
Plutocracy Paralyzed, ... 194

CHAPTER XXIX.
My Inaugural Message, ... 200

CHAPTER XXX.
Europe Prepares for War, ... 206

CHAPTER XXXI.
The Conquest of Canada, ... 208

CHAPTER XXXII.
The Conquest of Ireland, ... 210

CHAPTER XXXIII.
England's Surprise, ... 218

CHAPTER XXXIV.
Reconstructed Great Britain, ... 224

CHAPTER XXXV.
Sophie's Work, ... 228

CHAPTER XXXVI.
The Wrath of the Kings, ... 231

CONTENTS.

CHAPTER XXXVII.
The Battle of Marburg, ... 234

CHAPTER XXXVIII.
The Second Day of the Battle, ... 238

CHAPTER XXXIX.
The Third Day of the Conflict, ... 241

CHAPTER XL.
The Day of Jubilee, ... 244

CHAPTER XLI.
Armageddon, ... 253

CHAPTER XLII.
The Millennium, ... 264

CHAPTER XLIII.
Christianity, ... 269

CHAPTER XLIV.
The Universal Republic, ... 274

CHAPTER XLV.
We Prepare to Go Back to America, ... 278

CHAPTER XLVI.
We Visit England and Ireland, ... 282

CHAPTER XLVII.
America, ... 289

CHAPTER XLVIII.
The Sound of the Hammer, ... 294

CHAPTER XLIX.
My Last Visitor, ... 298

THE GOLDEN BOTTLE.

CHAPTER I.

WHO I AM, AND WHAT I THOUGHT.

I HAVE a wonderful story to tell.

But first—you ask—"who are *you?*"

Well, I am Ephraim Benezet, son of John Benezet and Mary his wife, of Butler County, Kansas.

It is the old, old story. Grasshoppers, poor crops, "pools," "trusts," "rings;" high prices for what we bought, low prices for what we sold; "burning the candle at both ends;" increasing taxation to support a lot of office-holding non-producers; an increasing family, with another lot of non-producers to support, much beloved, however, of their progenitors; debt, pinching economy, and, at last, that conditional sale of the homestead which is disguised under the name of a "mortgage." More debt to pay interest on, more pinching, more grasshoppers, more pools, more "combines," and the end—foreclosure—wiping out—starting adrift, etc.

I was the oldest son and not much of a help at that.

I was never physically strong: I had a tendency to pulmonary troubles, intensified by poor living and hopelessness. I was full of high dreams, a great reader, but of little real value to any one.

I had some thoughts at one time of studying for the ministry, for I had strong impulses to goodness; and I felt I was not equal to the labors of the farm. But then, as I beheld the wretchedness of mankind, universal and overwhelming; as I saw vice triumphant and virtue trampled under foot, the good cursed and the evil blessed, it seemed to me that it was not God but the devil who was ruling this wicked world. I used to go, in the night, and cry out in the open fields, under the stars, for God to come again on earth and make things right; and drive the victorious devils back into their sulphurous dens.

And then I reasoned it out that the great God, the Father Almighty, maker of the immeasurable universe, must be omnipotent and omniscient—that was conceded by all. Being omniscient he knew the condition of this misgoverned little planet; and being omnipotent he had the power to remedy it all, in the twinkling of an eye. And he did not do it. Why?

I could only explain it upon the theory that this world was not the direct creation of God, but the clumsy workmanship of a lot of spiritual beings, above men in power, but like unto them in infirmity; and that they had been set to work, by the divine command, and had been experimenting for a few million years to make something out of the elements committed to them; and had made a fearful muddle of it all. I thought I could also see that man was *their* deputy, to still further carry on this delegated work of creation, at second hand; and there was in man's evolution, for instance, of the locomotive, out of the log-wheeled wagon of Charlemagne, the same slow process, with the same imperfect adaptation of means to ends, which marked the evolution of man from a hairy simian; or the development of a humming-bird out of an alligator.

The Englishman's railroad car built in separate compartments, modelled exactly after the stage-coach of the last century, was very like the perpetuation, in man's body, of useless and often fatal inheritances from his animal progenitors. The one did not speak any more of omniscience and omnipotence than the other.

And so I worshipped, on bent knees, the sublime Architect of the Universe, the all-wise, all-powerful, and all-good, and called on him to listen to the cry of one of his poor little human creatures; and come to the aid of this perturbed planet, and whip his invisible spiritual agents into intelligence and righteousness, that good might rule on the earth and evil be banished into Hades.

But the stars listened to me, and winked their innumerable eyes at me, and answered not. And no reply came from behind the stars; and I fell into pitiful dejection and bitterness against all created things.

And my cough increased, and my heart was sore with sorrow.

For there was one fair girl, Sophie Hetherington by name, for whom my soul lamented. Years ago we sat beside each other on the same slab-bench, in the same old log school-house. She was fair and good and bright and affectionate. We trudged together through the snow in winter; we gathered flowers together in the woods in spring; we pelted each other with apples and nuts in the autumn. And the love which began in the little toddlers ripened to tenfold warmth in the growing manhood and womanhood.

Sophie's father was also a farmer. He owned the next farm to ours. He had caught the contagion of debt which overspread the State. He was a good, honest, intelligent, industrious man; but what can all such faculties effect when the thieves get in their robberies; when the heavens withhold their rainfall; when the demoniacal swarms of insects gather; and the clouds are sent hurtling away from the brazen heavens to pour down their load of moisture where it is not wanted? Oh! ye earth-spirits, are ye asleep; or do ye delight in the destruction of the honest and virtuous?

The blow at last fell. The Hetherington mortgage was foreclosed. One bright morning a pitiful *cortége* of grim-visaged men and weeping women went forth from that little paradise of fields and woods and prolific greenery, and took their sad way to the great city of Omaha, to struggle with thousands of hungry ones for daily food. And Sophie—bright, resolute, intellectual Sophie—became a store-girl at starvation wages, and stories began to come back to us—but enough! Her letters ceased, and my heart was blacker than midnight without a star. Oh, why! why! ye invisible, winged, deputy rulers of the globe, did not that rainfall come in time to save the crop and save Sophie?

And now it was our turn. Notice had been served that our mortgage would also be foreclosed.

No one spoke that night at supper. Mother was crying softly. Father looked the curses he did not speak. I sat at the foot of the table, furious at my own helplessness. The meagre meal was dispatched quickly. Our thoughts turned to the future. The future! It was like looking into the mouth of Hell. Oh, how many bitter hearts are there in this world!

I went out and talked to the stars as usual. But it was in vain. Useless was it to look to that quarter for help. I would go and hire out in the great city. But what could I do? The great city! The great maw that swallows up the wretchedness of the country and makes it greater. And then I had a fit of coughing. I stamped my foot on the earth and swore— yes, swore a bitter oath. I realized my own uselessness. I saw in the distance a pauper's grave. I could help no one, not even myself. More of the silly work of those wretched earth-spirits! In their reckless eagerness to create they had manufactured billions upon billions of microscopic forms of life, deadly to the life of man; and they had created man for the microbes to prey on and kill. I had a colony of them in my left lung, and they would breed and breed until they filled me and finished me. And these wretched earth-spirits took better care of the villanous, deadly, murdering bacilli than they did of me! Was I of no more consequence in the universe than these minute and wretched creatures? It seemed not. What was intellect worth if it could be thus overthrown by an army of animalculæ?

But there was nothing to be gained by pursuing such thoughts. I should go mad while thus flinging myself against the iron front of fate.

If I could do nothing else I could sleep.

And so I climbed the ladder to the loft and stretched myself upon my bed of straw. I knew every bare rafter above my head. I had studied them by daylight and moonlight and candle-light. I had woven my thoughts into the black timbers until every knot-hole seemed a piece of me. I knew they were there in the darkness. I could count them: one, two, three—as I had done a thousand times before.

I sighed. I set my teeth. I fell asleep—a dull, pained, unhappy sleep, with an under-current of cursing and bewailing.

CHAPTER II.

WHAT I SAW.

I THOUGHT I was awake. Now I know I was asleep and dreaming.

A light fell on my closed eyes and shone through the lids. I lifted up my head from the pillow.

What a curious sight!

There was an old man in the room. An old man with a broad brow, a smiling, gentle face, clear blue eyes and long gray hair; an aspect altogether benevolent and noble.

"Who are you?" I asked, for I thought him simply some human intruder.

In a clear, sweet voice he replied:

"THE PITY OF GOD."

The reply startled me. I had begun to think there was no pity in all the depths of the universe.

I sat up in the bed.

"What do you want?" I asked.

"SEE!" he replied.

He drew from his pocket a curious-looking embossed gold flask or bottle, and held it up before me.

"Yes," I replied, "what then?" For desperation and bitterness make men bold.

"OBSERVE," he said.

He pulled from the wall a large iron nail, which was used to hang clothes on. There was some water in a pitcher on the pine wash-stand, and a cup with a broken handle which I used for shaving. He poured the cup full of water, and then dropped the nail into it; there was just enough water to cover it. He stepped nearer to the bed, and held the cup sideways, so that I could look into it, and smiling at me, said:

"WATCH!"

He touched a spring in the neck of the golden flask and the top flew up, and he dropped just one drop of a clear, amber-colored liquid into the cup. There was an effervescence for a moment which clouded the water and hid the nail from sight.

Then he took the nail out and handed it to me. *It was as yellow as gold!*

The next instant he was gone, and the room was darkness. Where that light came from which had irradiated him I could never understand.

But it seemed to me that I went to sleep again.

CHAPTER III.

THE GOLDEN NAIL.

I WOKE at daybreak and looked around the loft, as it was revealed by the dim light—I coughed. All the horrors of my condition came back upon me. The foreclosure of the mortgage! Consumption! Death! And, worse than all, the injustice and cruelty of nature; the misery of the good, the happiness of the wicked. And Sophie gone—ruined!

I sat up in bed. My eyes were moist.

There was something in my hand.

It was a *golden nail!*

Yes; it looked like gold. I took it to the small window. Surely it *did* look like gold! But the light of dawn was dim, for we toilers rose early; the men who held the mortgages slept longer; but the mortgage worked all night, and so one thing equalized another. I lit a tallow candle and held the nail close to it.

Yes, it was the exact color of gold. I scratched it with my jack-knife. As far in as I cut it it was yellow; the color then was not a plating.

Suddenly my dream came back to me: the old man, the golden bottle, the transformed nail. This then was the nail; for he had handed it to me and I woke with it in my hand.

I gave a great start. Then my dream was something more than a gossamer figment of the troubled imagination.

I looked eagerly around the room. What is that lying on the foot of the bed, just where the old man stood when he gave me the nail? I darted forward.

I seized it. My God! it is the embossed flask out of which came that single drop which turned the rusty old iron nail into this semblance of shining yellow gold.

Stop! I pressed my hands to my throbbing head. I staggered under the rush of surging thoughts.

Could it be possible that this is the elixir for which the philosophers sought for a thousand years in vain? Do I hold in my hands the cure of all earthly poverty and the mastership of all worldly power?

I clutched the flask to my bosom.

Impossible, and yet—I am awake, *that* is certain. It is daylight. The vision of the old man may have been a dream, but here is the golden nail, here is the golden bottle. Nothing like these were ever seen before in this garret, nor in this house, nor in this neighborhood.

They are real. If the old man who called himself the "*Pity of God*" did not bring them here, whence came they?

And he showed me how to use the flask. I remembered that.

I shook it. It seemed to be nearly full.

I hugged it to my breast with more fervor than man ever embraced woman with.

But stop! What assurance have I that the flask will have, in my hand, the efficacy which it possessed in the grasp of my strange spiritual visitant? If it has not I am more wretched than ever, for I have had a glimpse of paradise, only to find the golden doors banged in my face.

But I can soon resolve that doubt.

I looked around the loft. Some children's clothes hung upon another nail. I threw them on the floor. I dragged the nail out—it took all my strength. Quickly I filled the cup with water, and placed the nail in it. Then I hunted for the spring in the neck of the flask. I found it. I pressed it. The lid flew open. My hand trembled so violently that it was some minutes before I could steady myself sufficiently to drop a single drop into the water. My soul was in my eyes. I trembled. I set the cup down on the wash-stand. I could not hold it.

There was a white effervescence which clouded the water; it foamed; then it cleared itself, and by the light of the candle I saw—*another golden nail!*

My God! How excited I was! I danced around the garret and upset the single backless chair, and the children in the next room wakened with the clatter.

But here there came upon me an appalling thought: What if these nails were not *real* gold? What if some ingenious demon was making sport of me? I stood still, paralyzed. My heart sank within me. I thought of the mortgage. My very hair stirred with terror.

There was one way to test it. The village of El Dorado was five miles distant. There was a jeweller there. He would tell me whether these nails were gold or not.

I dressed hurriedly. Mother was already up. Her tears were dropping into the pan of sizzling pork fat and rind-strings.

She looked at me and saw I was strangely disturbed.

"Ephraim," she said, "what's the matter?"

"Mother," I replied, "I have got an idea in my head, and I will take the gray mare and drive to El Dorado. I will be back at once."

She asked me questions; she offered me food; but I could neither answer nor eat. In a few minutes I was thundering down the road as fast as our fleetest horse could carry me.

Outside the town I stopped to calm myself. The jeweller was a lame man, named William Burke, with a leg which stuck out like a letter K; the rude boys called him "William with the side-draft." He was just opening his shop. He knew me.

"Good-morning, Mr. Burke," I said, with an affectation of calmness.

"Good-morning, Ephe," he replied; "how are all the folks?"

"Very well," I replied, "and yours?"

"Very well, thank you. Can I do anything for you this morning?"

"Yes," I said. "I ploughed up a couple of curious nails yesterday, and I thought I would drive over and see what they were worth."

He examined them. He filed into them. He applied acids. I watched him eagerly, my very knees knocking together.

"Well?" I said.

"Well," said he, "they are gold, of very pure quality."

"Sure?"

"Yes, perfectly sure."

My heart gave a great leap, and my face broke into smiles.

"You are in luck," he said.

I felt in the bosom of my coat to make sure that the flask had not disappeared.

"Yes," I replied, "great luck. What are they worth?"

He weighed them.

"Thirty-five dollars," he replied.

"Will you pay that for them?" I asked eagerly.

"Yes," he replied.

"Then take them," I said.

He paid me the money, and I ran out of the shop, leaving the jeweller looking after me, surprised and amused.

Lord! what visions opened before me!

Rich! Richer than Crœsus! Richer than any man

that had ever lived in this world. No more pinching, nor poverty, nor mortgages, nor broken hearts, nor ruined bodies. But Sophie! Ah! that was the rub. There are some things which even wealth cannot make good.

I went into a butcher-shop—then into a grocery store: meats, tenderloins, mutton-chops, the finest teas and coffees and chocolates, and canned goods, and candies for the children, and everything else I could think of. The news spread quickly, as it does in villages, and the merchants congratulated me on finding those curious evidences of the work of the Mound Builders (for that is the way in which they explained it), and laughed at my excitement, and the way I was loading up for the folks at home. The old gray mare was well burdened with sacks, and it was all I could do to hold them in place as we returned slowly to the farm.

But what delightful dreams I had! I did not cough once. Hope and joy had lifted me above the reach of the microbes. I had inherited the whole world, and I plotted and planned, until the road seemed paved with gold and the very fences had a yellowish hue as the old mare and I crawled past them.

I came in sight of the house. Father was sitting on the porch looking very depressed and melancholy.

I gave a yell that brought the whole family, including the dogs, out of the house with a rush.

"Give a hand here," I cried, as I lifted down the sacks.

We carried them in and emptied them on the kitchen table. The children danced for joy, but mother began to cry.

"What is the matter, mother?" I asked.

"Oh, Ephraim, Ephraim," she said, "I fear that in your desperation you have committed some crime."

"Do you think I stole these things?" I said, laughing.

"I fear you did, my son; how else could you get them?"

I roared with laughter.

"Come, mother," I said, "cook a royal breakfast for us all. Here is some of the Oolong tea you are so fond of, but you haven't had an ounce of it in the house for years. The money all went to fill the belly of that mortgage. I will pay off the mortgage to-morrow and we will never be poor again."

Father looked at me with open-eyed astonishment, as if he feared I had lost my senses.

"It is all true," I said; "our good luck has come at last—marvellous, extraordinary, incredible good luck. But hurry breakfast, send the children to school, and I will explain all."

The old house had never before smelt such fragrant odors as rolled through it and into every nook and crevice of it that bright morning. The very windows grew moist, like eyes overflowing with gratitude or strong drink.

I shall never forget the aroma of the coffee, for I

brought to it a ploughman's appetite and a palate not cloyed by surfeits.

When the children were all off, down the road to school, with their books under their arms, I pulled from my pocket the magical flask and told my story. No words can describe the astonishment of my parents.

They believed and yet they doubted; they doubted and yet they believed. How their eyes dilated and the wrinkles smoothed out as they looked into the glorious vista of the future, where there was to be no more debt, no more poverty. How the weight of the whole world was lifted from off their souls.

But I must prove my wonderful assertions before their very eyes.

This was at once done; and another golden nail was soon in their hands, to be weighed, examined, praised.

CHAPTER IV.

WE VISIT KANSAS CITY.

AND then we took counsel together.

The mortgage, that dreadful, devouring, insatiable, rapacious monster, that dragon of modern civilization, must be paid off. How?

After considerable conference it was agreed that I should make a dozen or more golden nails to sell to the jeweller; then we would take the team and wagon and go to El Dorado, sell them and buy a second-hand blacksmith's forge which I knew was in a certain tin-shop there for sale; and, with a supply of coal and bar-iron, we would forge brick-shaped masses, which I could convert into gold, and we would take them with us to Kansas City to sell.

This plan we carried out; and the next day half a dozen men were prowling around the farm; and that night we could see their lanterns as they dug away at an elevation, a sort of natural mound, in the middle of the field. They were towns-people. We laughed, but did not disturb them. They toiled all night, and in the morning we found quite an excavation where they had been laboring. They were looking for the Mound Builders' gold.

We set up the forge in a shed, and all the next day father and I worked the bellows and hammered and welded, until we turned out several large bricks of iron. We were clumsy workmen, but, Lord! how our blows rang, for hope and home were in every stroke.

It took but a few minutes to convert these iron masses into gold.

On the morrow we were off to Kansas City.

There we bought ourselves new suits of fashionable clothing, and then called on the principal jeweller of the city. We produced two bricks. He smiled a superior smile, as if he knew we were farmers who had been swindled by some "confidence game;" and to enlighten our ignorance he dropped a drop of *aqua fortis* on the face of one of the bricks. Instead of boiling up, angry and green, it lay there like a drop of water. He readjusted his spectacles and tried it again, with the same result. "Heavy plating," he muttered. He filed into it and tried the acid in the cleft. He summoned his master-workman from the back of the shop. They talked together in whispers. He turned to us.

"Have you any objection to my cutting through this brick?" he asked.

"None at all," I replied.

In a few minutes, with hammer and chisel and wedges, the brick was broken in half, and the acid applied to the edges. Still the same result. It lay there as harmless as water.

"This is gold," he said.

"Of course," I replied; "what did you take it for?"

He put the second brick through the same tests, with the same result.

We visited other jewellers' stores.

That night we had $55,800 in bank, with bank certificates of deposit for nearly that amount in our pockets, in sums of $1,000 each.

The mortgage on the farm was held by an English syndicate corporation, whose headquarters were in Kansas City; and the next morning we paid it off, and took a certificate of satisfaction. When father got that piece of paper in his pocket he stood straighter and looked more boldly before him than I had seen him do for years. The iron collar of servitude had been filed from off his neck with a file of gold.

I proposed to him that he buy a house in Kansas City and move his family there; but he would not hear of it. He had worked the fibres of his heart into the soil of that old place, and every tree and field and unpainted board was dear to him. I gave him certificates for $20,000; and we bought new furniture, china-ware, clothing, and everything that we could think would add to the pleasure and comfort of those at home.

We went to the principal and most expensive hotel.

What a glorious thing it was not to be obliged to count the pennies, as we had been doing all our lives. We went to the theatre. The stage was gay and glittering, but not half so much so as the pictures of the future which unrolled themselves before our happy eyes.

"Oh, Sophie! Sophie!" I said to myself, mournfully.

"Ephraim," said my father, at the most tragical part of the tragedy, "I think I will buy Hetherington's farm. It jines me on the west, you know, and it's for sale."

"Oh, Sophie, Sophie," I said to myself, "there is one thing money cannot do. It cannot restore woman's honor."

CHAPTER V.

RICH.

It is a delightful thing to feel rich. The difference between the mind of a wealthy man and that of a poor man is the difference between a room brilliantly lighted and one shrouded in darkness. In the first case every artistic form is revealed in the flood of illumination; in the other you bump your head against the walls and break your shins over the furniture; you grope, you crawl, you stumble, you swear.

These thoughts came to me as I sat on the thickly-cushioned, velvet-covered seat of the chair-car, looking out through the great plate-glass window of the railroad train at the variegated country flying rapidly past us.

At home I knew the history and circumstances of every family around me.

I could see through the flowers and the trees the miseries which every roof covered: the debt, the disappointments, the heart-burnings; the hopeless struggle against what they called fate, but which was simply man's incapacity to protect himself against human thieves, or to force unwilling nature to obey his commands. Hence the whole scene at home was a pitiful and melancholy one; the bright face of nature was changed to a sombre cast by the underlying human troubles. But how different were my feelings as we flew along in the cars, conscious that I possessed the means of illimitable wealth. I saw the possibilities, not the realities. In the unpainted house with the decaying porch, the rambling morning-glory vines, the neglected garden, and the tumble-down out-buildings, I saw the lordly and attractive mansion that might be, brilliant with gay colors and full of charming people. I planned out highways, railroads, villages, towns, cities, academies, universities as we whirled along; I forgot, for a time, the miseries of mankind in my own exaltation and happiness. My heart sang within me. There was but one black spot in all my thoughts, and across it in letters of fire was written the word "*Sophie.*"

Father was reading the morning paper, through his new gold-framed spectacles, in a chair next me. Suddenly he made an exclamation of surprise, and proceeded to peruse something intently.

"What is it?" I asked.

He handed me the paper, with his thumb at the top of a particular column. I read:

AN ASTONISHING AFFAIR—TWO MEN MADE SUDDENLY RICH.

Yesterday there arrived in town two farmer-looking men—roughly but cleanly dressed, and evidently father and son; the elder seemed to be about fifty or fifty-five years old, and the younger about twenty-two or twenty-three years of age.

Each of them bore a common carpet-bag. Their fellow-travellers on the railroad train did not imagine that these cheap sacks contained a large fortune.

The two travellers, after buying fashionable suits of clothes, proceeded to the celebrated establishment of Sutphin & Co., jewellers, and there produced two large-sized bricks of gold. Mr. Higgins, of the firm, at first thought that they were a couple of green farmers who had been tricked in the old-fashioned way by "confidence men," and that the bricks were simply lead with a gilt surface. And so he proceeded, smiling good-naturedly, as he tells us, to bore into one of them, but his astonishment was great to find that he was mistaken. Still suspicious, he asked permission to cut it in half; the farmers readily agreed to this; and when the brick was separated into two pieces and all the usual tests applied, it was demonstrated that it was really gold of extraordinary fineness and purity. The result was the strangers were paid the sum of $5,360 cash for the two bricks. Mr. Higgins was curious to know who the men were, and so while dispatching one of the clerks to follow them, he hurried to the office of the chief of police and had a detective put upon their track. They were found at the great jewelry establishment of Messrs. Burrows & Hogarty, where they sold two more bricks of gold for the sum of $4,823. The detective stood beside them while they made this sale, and was about to arrest them and compel them to account for how they came into possession of such valuable property, but he thought he would track them a little farther and see what they would do next. He followed them to other establishments, until they had sold gold bricks to the amount of $55,800. They proceeded then to the First National Bank, where they deposited $55,000, taking certificates of deposit for it, in the name of the younger man, Ephraim Benezet. They then went to the office of the Anglo-American Loan and Trust Company, and paid $1,272.50 in satisfaction of an overdue mortgage, given by John Benezet and Mary his wife, of Butler County, Kansas, upon one hundred and sixty acres of land in the vicinity of El Dorado, in that county. They then visited establishment after establishment, purchasing dry goods, furniture, jewelry, a carriage, pictures, etc., and ordered them boxed and shipped to the address of the elder man, at the town named, paying cash in every instance. The detective did not feel that he would be justified, under these cirumstances, in arresting such valuable customers of our leading merchants, and so, after shadowing the Benezets to their hotel, he reported all the facts to his chief. That officer heartily approved of his prudence and sagacity, and in the presence of the rest of the force thanked him, saying that these strangers, however they may have come by their wealth, were now rich men, and it would have been very unwise and improper to injure the trade of the city by offending them and forcing them to trade elsewhere; in fact, he said he hoped the members of his force would always remember that the rule of action which was proper and right when applied to penniless tramps could not be made to work where the suspected party was rich. Wealth had its privileges.

The chief then telegraphed the facts in the case to the chief of police of El Dorado, Kansas, and asked who the Benezets were, and how they came by the gold bricks. An answer was soon received, saying that they were, as was suspected, father and son; that they were honest, worthy, hard-working people, who lived on a farm a few miles from the town of El Dorado; that they had been very poor, in fact bankrupt, like most of their neighbors, and a mortgage on their farm had been placed quite recently in the hands of a local attorney to foreclose. A few days ago the younger Benezet had visited the town and sold two large gold nails, and bought household necessaries, of which the family was greatly in need. It was supposed that the young man in ploughing had turned up an ancient deposit, left there by some prehistoric civilization, possibly a branch of the Aztecs (this was the suggestion of Dr. Dunwoody, who was something of an antiquarian), and the "find" had created a great sensation; in fact, a number of the boys and business men of the town had gone out in the night to the farm, and dug over a large part of it, but without finding anything; and although they carrried lanterns, and must have been seen by the family, the Benezets made no attempt to drive them off the farm or to protect their supposed discovery. This was the report that came back from El Dorado.

The Benezets spent the night at the theatre in Kansas City, and seemed to enjoy the play very much. One of our reporters called to interview them, but they had retired for the night, after inquiring of the clerk the hour at which the morning train left for their home.

LATER.—As we go to press a telegram is received from the editor of the *Trumpet of Freedom*, of El Dorado, asking for five hundred words of a report of all the details of the actions of the Benezets while in Kansas City. The news of their sudden wealth has produced the wildest excitement in that little town; all business is practically suspended; the whole populace has turned out on the streets; and at every corner buzzing crowds of eager talkers and listeners are gathered discussing the extraordinary news. There was talk of adjourning to the court-house to hold a meeting, but at three o'clock the cry was raised: "To the farm! To the farm!" In ten minutes the whole town was deserted, except by the children and a few sick people. The crowd swarmed in carriages, buggies, lumber-wagons, and on foot—an excited cavalcade of men, women, girls, and boys, all pushing forward, full of curiosity and expectation. When the head of the tumultuous procession reached the farm they found no one at home but poor old Mrs. Benezet, who is in feeble health. She was in the kitchen, at work, when they overwhelmed her with the news and plied her with a thousand questions. The leading citizens, the lawyers, and clergymen were civil enough in their inquiries, but the rest swarmed into every part of the house, took possession of the spades, shovels, hoes, and crowbars, and were soon at work digging up the cellar and the garden, and every other spot where they thought the rest of the wonderful gold bricks might be concealed.

But the search was entirely in vain. There were no signs of a gold mine, or an Aztec temple, or even a mound-builder's mound on the place. The visitors excavated the floor of the cellar to the depth of six feet, and the garden was ruined, heaped up in piles and ridges, but not a scrap of gold was found. Mrs. Benezet, if she knew anything, refused to tell it. Diligent inquiry among the neighbors did not reveal that any missing traveller had passed through that neighborhood, whose murder might have accounted for the sudden wealth of the Benezets. In fact, the whole population are at their wits' end to find some explanation of this extraordinary accession of wealth by a family whose appearance indicated nothing but extreme poverty. It is said that very few of the people of the town of El Dorado or vicinity will sleep a wink to-night. At eleven o'clock they are gathered in mobs in all the principal stores, their numbers increased by multitudes of farmers, for the news has spread with wonderful rapidity all through the country. The wildest suggestions are made. The general belief is that the Benezets have found an Aztec temple of solid gold, and that the bricks are but a trifling part of the whole "find." Some propose that when the Benezets return they be put to the torture, and compelled to reveal the location of the temple, or the mine, or whatever it is. The feeling of every man is that he must have part of that gold; their eyes shine with a wild light that is dangerous. The farmers especially are desperate, and they cannot understand why the Benezets should carry off that immense fortune while they are unable to pay their taxes or the interest on their mortgages. Indeed, it may be said that nothing has happened, since the firing on Fort Sumter, many years ago, that has occasioned so tremendous an excitement in this county as the news telegraphed here yesterday by the Chief of Police of Kansas City.

"Well, Ephe," said father, when I laid down the paper, "what do you say to that?"

"I am very much astonished," I replied. "Two days ago we could have starved to death in the streets of Kansas City, and a three-line notice, in the smallest type, in an obscure corner of a newspaper, would have been all the notice given of us. Here we have two whole columns, with great head-lines, and our every action observed and detailed."

"But, Ephe," said my father, "if they are going to mob us, and hang us up by the neck, and lower us down, and haul us up again, until we tell your secret, and they take the 'golden bottle' away from you, we had better turn back, send for your mother and the family, and sell the place at auction."

"Well," I replied, "I don't think they will do anything of the kind. You couldn't get a mob of average American citizens to hang a rich man. They worship money more than they do their God. It is the Moloch of their idolatry."

Just then the train hauled up at a little station and a crowd of villagers poured into the car. They conversed with the brakeman and I saw him pointing us out. They rushed up to us, and one said:

"Misters, be ye the men what found the Aztec gold mine? Where——"

But just then the conductor bawled "all aboard!" the train started with a jolt, and the excited intruders scampered off, like rats, jumping to the platform full of disappointed curiosity.

It seemed to me that every one on the train stalked through our car to stare at us. A smooth-faced, white-collared clergyman, all smiles, benevolence, and rubbings-of-hands, opened conversation and the crowd gathered around us. But it was not a rude crowd; indeed, it was deferential and obsequious; they looked through us and saw our bank account, and, in the distance, they perceived dimly the buried Aztec temple, or the hidden gold mine, or whatever it was;

and they were all smiles and attention. Not a word that we uttered was lost upon them; the simplest phrase about the weather sank deep into their inner consciousness, to be treasured in their memories and repeated for months, as oracular and profound utterances, brighter than diamonds, weightier than gold.

After a few commonplace remarks about the crops and the seasons, my reverend friend first explained that men of his cloth always have their thoughts—very properly—fixed on the things of another and better world (this with elongated jaw and a sigh); yet he confessed that, being merely human, they possessed the natural curiosity of their species, and he had read, with profound interest, the report in the morning papers of our great discovery, and would like to ask us a few questions.

I answered his inquiries politely enough, rambling off upon collateral matters, but giving him no information which he did not already possess. It was a very pretty game of parry and thrust, and it was interrupted by the brakeman crying out the name of another town, larger than the last.

"Look at the crowd!" cried one of the passengers.

The depot platform was black with people.

The brakeman was kept busy pointing us out. The villagers broke into the car; they flattened their noses against the windows; and then some cried: "Benezet! Benezet! Speech! speech!"

At every station the crowds increased and the excitement became greater. The conductor at length requested us to step to the platform and satisfy the natural curiosity of the people. Lord! how they shouted when we appeared, and they pushed forward by the hundred to shake hands. Some were moved by the simple admiration which mere wealth creates; others saw in us possibilities that dilated their hearts, for had we not been, like themselves, poor struggling men, up to the ears in debt, and had we not, by a sudden turn of the wheel of fortune, achieved independence of poverty and the money-lenders? I was forced to speak a few words to them at every station.

And here a curious transition was gradually worked within me. My only thought, when I realized that I held, in the golden bottle, the source of immense wealth, was that I would lift my family and myself out of wretchedness. I had visions of comfort, joy, the luxuries of life, books, music, pleasant society, travel, culture, everything that goes to delight the heart of man. But when I looked out over those swarming multitudes, with their hot eyes and eager, drawn faces, and read in them the same old story of unending struggle with untoward circumstances, my heart went out to them, and I resolved to do all in my power to help them and make mankind nobler and happier. And something of this must have burned in my words and shone in my face, for the cheers were vociferous. And so from town to town our progress was a continuous ovation.

CHAPTER VI.

GOING HOME.

FATHER grew more and more uneasy as we drew near the town of El Dorado. He could not forget those suggestions about putting us to the torture.

"Why," said he, "it is in the power of that villanous editor of the *Trumpet of Freedom* to rouse the people up to mob us!"

"Don't have any fear on that point," I replied. "I have here, in my pocket-book, two little clippings from that worthy's paper. I cut them out because they were the first occasions when I was referred to in public print. Just read them, and they will show you how the possession of wealth is likely to affect that gentleman. Here is the first one."

I handed him a little slip which contained these words:

CURIOUS.

It has not been generally supposed that Kansas possessed any relics of a civilized race dwelling here before the whites took possession of the country, but yesterday Mr. William Burke, our popular jeweller, whose advertisement will be found in another column, purchased of a farmer boy, named Ephe Benezet, two objects which will go far toward establishing a different conclusion. They were two gold nails, each about four inches long, shaped very much like old-fashioned wrought-iron nails, showing even the marks of the hammer with which they were made. The gold was of the finest quality. The boy said he had found them in ploughing. He is a long-legged, ignorant, gawky fellow, too lazy to work to help his old father out of debt, but given (so the neighbors say) to lying around and reading trashy books. It is supposed that his story is true and that he ploughed these nails up, and that they are relics of some by-gone age. Some of our scientists should obtain them and not let them be put into the melting-pot.

The second notice appeared after the sale of the second and larger batch of nails. The tone of the paper had visibly changed. It read as follows:

IMPORTANT.

With our usual enterprise we gave the public in our last issue an account of the sale of two golden nails to Mr. William Burke, the well-known jeweller of this city (his advertisement will be found on our fourth page). Since then we have to record that the same young man, Mr. Ephraim Benezet, son of that worthy gentleman, Mr. John Benezet, who lives five miles from town, has returned and sold Mr. Burke twenty-one more golden nails. The amount of the sale was $480. This is really startling and important news, and may be of great importance to the people of this section. It would look as if the Benezet family had stumbled on a fortune. It is suggested by some of our excited townsmen that they have found a buried temple of the old Aztec sun-worship on their farm, every part of it being pure gold. If such a suggestion should prove true there may be similar remains on other farms—yes, beneath this very town! The young gentleman, Mr. Ephraim Benezet, who has on both occasions brought in the golden objects to sell, is a young man of fine intelligence and a great student—a credit, indeed, to Butler County.

Our people are very much excited over the news, and we

hope to have fuller details in our next issue. We shall devote special attention to the matter. Now is a good time to subscribe for the *Trumpet of Freedom*. Remember our terms, one dollar a year, invariably in advance. The best paper in the county, with a larger circulation than any other; don't forget our motto: "neutral in all things, independent in nothing."

"Do you think," I said to my father, "that the fellow who ascended the scale of adulation as rapidly as that will lead a mob to hang us when he hears of our great wealth? No, no! there is no danger of it."

At a station, just before we reached the town of El Dorado, a newsboy ran into the car, crying:

"Here's a copy of the extra *Trumpet of Freedom*. Full account of the discovery of a gold mine and a statute of the sun!"

I bought a copy and found the whole first page filled with a glowing article about ourselves and the gold mine. Nothing had been omitted that ingenuity or industry could scrape together to satisfy the insatiable curiosity of the public. There was a long telegram from Kansas City, together with summaries of the editorial comments of the various Kansas City newspapers. There was a full account of the ancient Aztec civilization. There were portraits of our whole family; the one of myself being especially handsome and conspicuous. There was an account of our pedigree, dating back to the *Mayflower;* and a glowing biography of my mother's great-granduncle, who was a sutler's clerk in the Revolutionary War. There was also a picture of our tumble-down house, touched up to look like quite a handsome mansion; and there, too, was our poor old fly-bitten bull, a most demure and harmless creature, represented as rampaging down a forty-acre field, with head up and tail perpendicular, looking for all the world like a wild and ferocious *aurochs* in a Muscovite forest. The touch of gold had beautified our faces, our dwelling, our characters, our pedigree, our stock, and even our poultry; for the hens and roosters looked as if they might have taken the first premium at every agricultural fair in Kansas for the last twenty years. The whole first page was nothing but BENEZET—BENEZET—BENEZET, until the eye wearied of it. Silly stories were told to illustrate what a great and illustrious family we were; and I was boldly proclaimed to be the ablest young man in ten counties. The editor was down on his stomach and crawling all over the ground in circles, on his vest buttons, and rubbing his nose in the mire before the august spectacle of those gold bricks and the awful possibilities that lay behind them. He fairly shrieked with ecstatic headlines, and big type that seemed to stand on the very tiptoe of exultation.

THEY ARE COMING!
THEY LEFT KANSAS CITY AT NINE O'CLOCK THIS MORNING!
THEY WILL REACH HERE AT FOUR O'CLOCK AND THIRTY-TWO MINUTES!
THE COMMON COUNCIL APPOINTS A COMMITTEE TO MEET THEM! A BANQUET THIS EVENING AT THE COURT-HOUSE! SPEECHES AND MUSIC, ETC.

"There, old gentleman," I said, as father read the paper over my shoulder, "does that look like hauling us up and letting us down again, and then hauling us up again, till we tell where the Aztec temple is?"

Father smiled a complacent smile.

"Ephe," he said, "isn't it wonderful! Just to think; these people would have let the whole caboodle of us starve to death out on the old farm, and never held out a hand to help us. They would have seen that mortgage foreclosed, and you and me and the old woman and all the rest of us driven out on the public highway, with no more pity than they have felt for the thousands of other honest farmers who have been squeezed off the face of the land during the last twenty years in Kansas."

"Dad," I said, for that was my familiar way of addressing my honored father at times, "did you ever read Shakespeare?"

"No," he replied, "I can't say I did."

"Well," I said, "you can't begin too soon, for you are a rich man now, and culture and wealth always go together in America. A rich man who wasn't a Shakespearean scholar would be a great curiosity in the United States. Well, there is a play called 'Hamlet,' which it is said Shakespeare wrote. *Hamlet* has an uncle, a measly old villain, a scaly-looking old 'cuss' who kills his brother by putting patent medicine in his ear, and then becomes king; and young *Hamlet* philosophizes upon the way in which the multitude get down on their bellies and wriggle in the mud before his uncle, just as these chaps are doing before us, and he says:

"'It is not strange; for my uncle is king of Denmark, and those that would make mows at him while my father lived, give twenty, forty, an hundred ducats apiece for his picture in little. 'Sblood, there is something in this more than natural, if philosophy could find it out.'

"I tell you, dad, human nature is the meanest thing on the planet; and we mustn't lose our heads or be carried away by the flatteries of the crowd; for I have no doubt that if a telegram came from Kansas City saying that those bricks which we sold yesterday had turned out to be brass, the same fellows who are gathering to give us an ovation would hang us with equal spirit and unanimity. The rich man should never forget that the honors which accompany him are not paid to himself, but to his money; and without it he would not be of any more account than a half-naked tramp. If they could get that idea into their heads it would knock the nonsense out of them. Of themselves they are nothing."

I had to read the old gentleman this lecture, for I perceived he had already begun to perk himself up, and swell and carry his chin an inch higher than I had ever seen it before: and when he spoke of the "common people," there was a something in his tone which indicated loftiness and distance, as if he were talking from a mountain top down into a valley. I very much fear that success is going to turn the old gentleman's head. For my part, whether my good sense is stronger or my memory better, I cannot forget the past in the present.

But here we are at the station. Lord! what a crowd! The whole town, men, women, and children, had turned out to do us honor. And what a roar of cheers and banging of drums and braying of trumpets as we stepped out. And when the multitude caught sight of our broadcloth suits, and high silk hats, and new yellow leather valises, silver-plated, they roared again, louder than ever; for these were the visible confirmations and outward signs and tokens of the marvellous story told by the telegraphic wires. The latter they had heard, but here they saw, with their very eyes, the men who had departed in rough garb coming back clothed in a glory unknown to Solomon; for silk hats were unheard of among "the chosen people," although their descendants have dealt extensively in them since—that is, ripe ones. The Lord did a great deal for the Jews, but he did not vouchsafe to them the glistening, cylindrical, glorious head temples of our modern civilization; the tiles which, in every other country but the barbaric West, mark the distinction between the gentleman and the mere man.

The leading lawyer of the town (the miseries and follies of the people sustained three or four of these representatives of trained and acute intellect), a fellow by the name of Spooner—one of the devil's "long spoons," a cadaverous, lengthy, black-jawed, hard-faced, wolfish-looking creature, with ten times a wolf's ferocity and appetite for spoil; a man I utterly loathed, for he was most merciless plunderer of the poor and distressed in the whole country— stepped forward to deliver the speech of welcome. He was quite a stringer-together of words, but his verbiage had no more connection with his heart or conscience than the sea-weed of "the Sargasso sea" has with the bottom of the ocean on whose top it floats.

"Illustrious men!" he began, "you left us, as it were, but yesterday, unknown and obscure; you return world-famous to the bosoms of the people who love you and are proud of you." (Great cheering.) "You return as Columbus did to Spain, bearing with him the golden treasures (immense cheering) of the new world. You return to bring, as we fondly hope, a new era of unprecedented prosperity to this——" the rest of the sentence was lost in the uproar of the excited populace, but through it I could see the human-wolf waving his arms wildly, the sweat pouring in streams from his ugly face.

There was no use of any more oratory (the rest of the noble oration, two columns in length, appeared in the next issue of the *Trumpet of Freedom*), but the impatient crowd could not be restrained; they rushed forward to embrace and shake hands with my father and myself. I thought they would "kill us with kindness;" in the crush one woman fainted; a corpulent dry-goods merchant was flattened out until he looked as if he had passed through a clothes-wringer, and a boy had his leg broken; while my right arm was worked like a pump-handle until it was sore for a week afterward.

But at last, surrounded by the swarming, surging, yelling, admiring mob, we fought our way to the principal hotel, where the best rooms had been engaged for us. It was one o'clock the next morning before the last of the enthusiastic mob dispersed, and the streets around the hotel resumed their usual peaceful midnight quiet.

The next day the furniture, the carpets, the carriage, the dry goods, etc., began to arrive, and the enthusiasm redoubled. The whole town went wild. No one suggested that we ought to have bought those goods at home. The truth is, as I soon discovered, in America a rich man, like the king of England under the common law, "can do no wrong." I was really ashamed to read the fulsome praises of myself in the next issue of the *Trumpet of Freedom*. According to the worthy editor Cicero was an imbecile, as an orator, compared with me; as a philosopher Sir Isaac Newton and Charles Darwin were nowhere; as a philanthropist (I had not yet done a single thing to deserve the good opinion of mankind), Wilberforce, Girard, and Peabody were not to be mentioned in the same hour. My lightest expressions were taken up and used as the text for editorials, and marvellous and recondite meanings were found in them, which I myself had never dreamed of. Really, I do not wonder that the very wealthy trample upon mankind; for they find the whole world, except a few noble and isolated souls, prostrate on the earth beneath their feet; they can't move without treading on some surrendered human right or some obsequious, cringing human body.

And I said to myself: if all this adulation comes from the possession of the comparatively small fortune which I possess, what would these creatures say if they knew I carried in the breast-pocket of this coat a fortune much greater than all the accumulated wealth of all the world? Why, they would simply die from an utter and absolute collapse of servility! They would perish out of an illimitable access of baseness!

CHAPTER VII.

I BEGIN WORK.

Now all this time there had been a strong sentiment turbulently at work in my heart; it was a sentiment of great pity for the wretches who suffered, as we had suffered, but the other day. I recalled, with vivid distinctness, my own feelings, as I lay there and looked at the bare rafters of that garret, and counted the knots—the unutterable woe of poverty closing in upon me, above, around me, as if the blue heavens had turned into iron, and were slowly descending to crush me and grind me into the earth. And I thanked God that I possessed the telescopic power to see through the planetary distance which separated my soul from the soul of my neighbor; and to remember his miseries in the midst of my own happiness. And yet—I said to myself—let no man take any pride in any good quality he may possess; for no man ever made the ten-thousandth part of himself; and everything that is admirable in him is not of the dust, the lime, the sand, the phosphorus; but it is a shedding of the spirit of goodness from the external spiritual world: a part of the prompting that keeps the uni-

I BEGIN WORK.

verse in motion. And this, I felt, was especially so in my case. The Influence which had sent that strange old man—the "*Pity of God*"—to me, with the "Golden Bottle," was no doubt filling my heart with the impulses which were to color my whole life. I was impelled, as all are, to the appointed work of life.

And so I first hunted up a lawyer of the town named Archibald M. Hayes. He was originally from one of the New England States—New Hampshire, I think. He was a fair-haired, pleasant-faced, genial, honest man, full of kindly thoughts toward his fellows. He was not a man-hunter; and, as a result, he was poor; for in our Western towns the people are like shipwrecked mariners on desert islands; every man is ready to eat his fellows; and the amount of his substance is usually symbolic of the number he has devoured. The village capitalist is like the sailor in the "Bab Ballads," who had cannibalized the whole crew of the *Nancy Bell*, and who thus tells his grewsome story:

> "And I never larf, and I never smile,
>   And I never lark nor play;
> But I sit and croak, and a single joke
>   I have—which is to say:
>
> 'Oh, I am a cook, and a captain bold,
>   And the mate of the Nancy brig,
> And a bo'sun tight, and a midshipmite,
>   And the crew of the captain's gig.'"

There are, of course, in every community noble

exceptions; but what Young wrote in his "Night Thoughts," of the conditions in England two or three generations ago, is true to-day of all parts of the United States.

> "Eager ambition's fiery chase I see;
> I see the circling hunt of noisy men,
> Burst law's enclosure; leap the mounds of right;
> Pursuers and pursued, each other's prey
> Till Death—that mighty hunter—earths them all."

I asked Mr. Hayes if he knew of any parties whose homes had been foreclosed on, but who still had the right to redeem them.

"Oh, yes!" he replied, "there are hundreds of them."

I handed him five hundred dollars.

"What is this for?" he asked.

"It is a retaining fee for yourself," I replied. "I propose to do some good in the world; and I want an honest and intelligent man to help me. I propose that you shall at once find every farmer or mechanic who has lost his home, but whose redemption period has not yet expired, and advance him the money to save his property, on ten or twenty years' time, at two per cent per annum."

Mr. Hayes rose to his feet, pushed the hair back from his forehead, and looked at me wildly, intently, and with alarm.

"Pardon me, my dear sir," he said, "I don't want to insult you—but—but—are you in your right mind? It would take more money than you are worth, many times over, to carry out your proposal; and to lend money at *two* per cent, when it is worth from ten and a bonus up to forty per cent, is—pardon the expression—insanity!"

And he pushed the five hundred dollars across the table to me.

"I do not want to take advantage of a temporary aberration of your mind," he said firmly, but quite respectfully.

"My dear sir," I replied, "I am glad to see that you are as honest as report gives you out. You must help me to do the good I contemplate. You need have no fears about the extent of my fortune. I will undertake to pay off every mortgage in Kansas —we may come to that in time—but at present I simply propose to help the poor fellows who are under the harrow in this my own county. They can never get out of debt paying the rates of interest they do, but with loans at two per cent per annum they can. And really, I would not care if they never paid me a penny of principal or interest; but I know that most of them are too proud to accept a gift outright, and therefore I propose to help them with loans, on their own time, at low rates of interest."

Mr. Hayes' astonishment, expressed in every line of his face, was unbounded. He still had his doubts about my sanity; but my manner was so calm, and my assurances so positive, that he could not help but accept my statements, though with many misgivings; and at last he reluctantly took the money I had placed before him. He left me to go to the office of the register of deeds to make out a list of the homesteads foreclosed upon within the past year.

I said to him at parting:

"Come to me at once if there are any cases that need immediate action."

CHAPTER VIII.

THE THUNDERBOLT.

I WALKED to the office of the *Trumpet of Freedom*, and wrote out and handed the editor, with a five dollar bill, the following advertisement. I shall never forget the unbounded astonishment with which he read it. He looked at me wildly and edged around until he got near the iron poker, with the stove between us.

"Do not be alarmed," I said quietly; "I am perfectly sane and harmless."

My manner reassured him somewhat.

"But two per cent per annum! Great heavens!" he cried, "no sane man can propose to lend money in Kansas at two per cent per annum. Why, my dear sir, the United States Treasury could not supply the demand! Two per cent per annum! Why, only this morning, Banker Smithers was wondering how you would invest your money, and he said to me he could put you onto a lay that would yield you forty-five per cent per annum. He is going to talk to you about it."

"Forty-five per cent!" I cried. "There is no

man in Kansas can pay such a rate. It simply means ruin to the borrower, and the transfer of the property of the many into the hands of the few; the reduction of the people to serfdom, and the overthrow of our free institutions. Why, the farmers cannot pay ten per cent; no, nor eight, nor six per cent. The mortgaged farm is, in nine cases out of ten, a lost farm."

The editor's eyes opened very widely.

"These are extraordinary views for a rich man to hold," he said; "I should expect to hear them at a meeting of crazy, Farmer-Alliance cranks, or at an assemblage of Knights of Labor; but for a wealthy man, whose first instinct should be to increase his fortune, they are extraordinary. What business is it of yours what becomes of the borrowers?"

"Business of mine?" I replied warmly; "it is my business that this country be not depopulated; that families be not broken up by poverty, and driven to evil lives by wretchedness; it is my business that humanity be not degraded into beastliness, and liberty made a mockery and a reproach. But do you decline my advertisement?"

"Not at all," he replied quickly, coming forward from behind the fortification of the stove; "indeed it is none of my business what you do with your money; but I could not help giving you a little good advice."

The next day the advertisement appeared. It read as follows:

NOTICE.

I am prepared to loan money on real estate security, in city or country, in this county occupied as homes, on from one to twenty years' time, as the borrower may prefer, at *two (2) per cent per annum*, without bonus of any kind. I am also ready to advance money, at the same rate, to parties whose homes have been foreclosed upon, but who still have an equity of redemption in the same. I will also advance to any person who has lost his homestead the money to buy it back, when he is able to do so, on the same terms as above. All parties will apply to Archibald M. Hayes, who will arrange all the details and pay over the money.

EPHRAIM BENEZET.

A thunderbolt falling out of a clear sky, and tearing the Court House, at one stroke, into "inch bits," could not have created greater astonishment than this simple little advertisement. If highwaymen had raided the town, and emptied all the banks, the indignation could not have been greater among the business men.

The news spread. It flew like electricity from house to house. The general verdict was that I was as crazy as a March hare, and that my money would not hold out; and the unfortunate debtors flocked into town, each one hurrying to get a dip into my purse before it was exhausted. The street around Mr. Hayes' office swarmed with a mighty multitude, fighting, wrangling, pushing, swearing, screaming, to get at the bewildered attorney, who, with six clerks to help him, was registering the applications in their order, as fast as they could be taken down.

That night—or rather the next morning—at one o'clock, there came a rapping at my bed-room door in the hotel, not loud enough to awaken the adjoining sleepers, but a persistent and gentle tapping. I opened the door and Mr. Hayes entered. I lighted the lamp. I found my visitor looking very pale and flurried.

"What is the matter?" I asked.

"The bankers, and in fact all the business men," he said, "are terribly excited. Your course will destroy their business. Merchants, doctors, lawyers, clergymen, in fact all parties, charge high rates of interest on every dollar due them: you are smashing everything. They held a meeting this afternoon, and Spooner—the fellow who made that speech of welcome to you—has prepared the papers, and to-morrow morning you are to be arrested on a charge of insanity, and sent to the Insane Asylum; and once there they will have political influence enough to keep you there for years. The worst of it is, that they have seen your father and worked upon him, and he agrees that you are crazy, and are about to squander the fortune which properly belongs to your family; and he is to be here to-morrow to help them, and the proceedings are to be instituted in his name."

"But I shall defend myself," I said.

"Defend yourself!" he cried, "why, there isn't a jury in Kansas that would not convict any man of insanity who would lend money at two per cent per annum, when he could get twelve to fifty per cent."

"What can I do?" I asked.

"You must get out of this at once. I have a fast horse and buggy, and a good driver at the corner, who will take you out of the county before sun-up, and leave you at a distant railroad station."

"You are very kind," I said; "I will follow your advice. But we must not give up the good work. You must continue taking applications, and I will send you drafts from New York."

"There it goes again!" he cried, throwing up his hands in despair. "Don't talk that way! Here are the five hundred dollars you gave me. Why, man alive! the applications now amount to over two hundred thousand dollars. I worked until twelve o'clock, and they are sleeping on the door-steps and all over the pavement by hundreds, waiting to get at me early in the morning. No; I can go no farther in the matter. It has ruined my profession already. The business men are fierce against me. I have a wife and family to support. I must take care of them."

"How much do you earn a year?" I asked.

"About twelve hundred dollars," he replied blushing, for I think he exaggerated somewhat.

"Here," I said, "are certificates of deposit for five thousand dollars. See, I indorse them to your order. I employ you for one year. If that is not enough, let me know."

He was very much astonished, but took the certificates of deposit.

"And here," I added, "are drafts for eight thousand dollars more. Use them in the most pressing cases, and I will send you from New York all the money you may need. My first remittance will be for two hundred thousand dollars in gold, by express, for I cannot trust these bankers. Do not fear; my means are simply unlimited. I do not propose to be stopped in my efforts to relieve the unfortunate by a gang of usurers."

I dressed quietly. We slipped downstairs together on tip-toe. I bade him good-by, and by morning I was on the cars steaming rapidly to New York.

CHAPTER IX.

DOING BUSINESS ON A LARGE SCALE.

On the cars, as I proceeded eastward, I bought the daily papers. There were in them numerous references to myself. I remember one article which read something like this:

EXTRAORDINARY IF TRUE.

A very singular circumstance has happened at the town of El Dorado, in Butler County, Kansas; we have already had occasion to refer to it, in part, in our dispatches. A hardworking, bankrupt farmer of that neighborhood, and his son, appeared at Kansas City recently and sold a number of bricks, of solid gold, to jewellers for $55,000. There was no question about the reality of the gold; it was of exceptional purity, and did not contain nearly as much alloy as the ordinary gold of commerce; but the wonder was where the two men could have found such a treasure. At first it was thought they had stumbled upon some prehistoric city or temple, or had discovered a gold mine; but diligent examination of their farm, and, in fact, of the whole neighborhood, revealed no deposit of the kind; there was, indeed, nothing to be found upon the farm but the ordinary clay and loam of a Kansas prairie, and a few shabby buildings. Our readers will remember our telegraphic reports of the excitement, in the little town of El Dorado, when the denizens of that burg received the Benezets—that is the name of the farmer and his son—with open arms on their return home; and the dining and wining and speech-making, in true

Western style, which followed. It does not take much to make a demigod in one of those frontier towns in the wild and woolly West; if a commonplace man builds a street-car line, with borrowed capital, or introduces electric lights, or even erects a block of buildings, he shares with Divinity the adoration and homage of the people; in fact, he has rather the best of it, for the populace worship God only on Sundays, and that in a perfunctory manner, and principally through the women; while men and women prostrate themselves before the real or alleged capitalist every day in the week, with a sincerity which cannot be questioned. We are glad to know that this servile adulation of mere wealth does not prevail in this region, where millionaires are as plentiful as blackberries.

But we have now some still more startling news by telegraph from the town of El Dorado. It seems that the real owner of the gold bricks, and consequently of the secret of their discovery, was not the elder Mr. Benezet, but the younger man, his son Ephraim; and he, it seems, has just played a caper which has astonished and paralyzed all Kansas. He has actually offered to loan money enough to pay off all the farm-mortgages in Butler county, and redeem all the foreclosed homesteads therein, and advance money to the farmers to buy back all the farms that they had lost by mortgage sales, and wait twenty years for his money at *two per cent per annum!* When it is understood that the ordinary Kansas money-lender expects to make from twenty to sixty per cent per annum on his capital—according to the elasticity of his conscience—the extraordinary nature of this proposition can be imagined. Strange to say, Ephraim Benezet disappeared suddenly from the town of El Dorado last night. Where he went no one knows. He did not leave by rail, for the bankers were waiting to arrest him as a lunatic. He dropped out of sight as utterly as if the earth had swallowed him. But, strangest of all, before he left he employed a well-known lawyer of the town, for the large salary of five thousand dollars per year, to represent him in redeeming land sold under mortgage foreclosures, and left eight thousand dollars with him for a beginning. Over two hundred thousand dollars of loans have already been engaged at two per cent per annum. Great excitement prevails. It is evident that Ephraim Benezet did not derive his wealth from any deposit on his father's farm, for he never went near it after his return to El Dorado ; and how this poor farmer's boy could suddenly develop into the possessor of a large fortune, and pay five thousand dollars to a lawyer to make contracts that may aggregate a million dollars, no one can understand. The natural conclusion would be that the man was insane; but the gold bricks, and the five thousand dollars to the lawyer, and the large sum of fifty-five thousand dollars deposited in the Kansas City bank, are not to be explained in that way. One is reminded of the stories of the Middle Ages— of the philosopher's stone, which turned baser metals into gold. The public will watch the developments of this business with great curiosity and interest. But, in the mean time, what has become of the mysterious philanthropist, Ephraim Benezet?

The whole thing reads like a fairy-tale.

I perused this with great attention. I saw that I could not hereafter avoid publicity. I perceived also that the Aztec temple and the gold mine would no longer serve my purpose. I should have to boldly declare that, by a series of chemical experiments, I had discovered the universal solvent; the philosopher's stone; the power of making gold. And with that announcement all modesty and privacy were out of the question: I should become at once the centre of attraction for the whole world. If the actual truth was known, I would be murdered for the possession of the magic bottle; but scientific knowledge was something that could not be taken from the dead man's head by the assassin. To do the good I contemplated, I must practise certain deceptions on the public; I must perplex them with a chemical laboratory, and all sorts of acids and alkalies, so as to uphold the delusion that I had indeed discovered the great solvent—the philosopher's stone—claimed to have been possessed by Paracelsus and Albertus Magnus.

As my gold bullion had to be turned into government coins at the United States Mint, I came to the conclusion that I had better establish myself in Philadelphia, where such an institution existed, so as to save, as far as possible, the anxieties and worries of the transportation of the precious metal.

And so, after stopping a day or two to view the wonders of New York, which I saw for the first time, I passed on to the Quaker City. A few days found me established in a handsome house on a quiet street, in a refined neighborhood. I engaged servants, bought horses and carriages, furniture, books, etc. One can live in the city of Penn with as much quiet comfort as he can anywhere in the world; the people are hospitable and cultured, and there is in the very atmosphere a gentle dignity and refinement which seems to be a survival from the days when it was the nation's capital, and stood at the fore-front of the newly liberated colonies.

There was what they call a basement kitchen to my house, one-half of which was above the level of the street. I fitted this up as my laboratory. I bought a number of mysterious looking retorts; I had a furnace of bricks built in one corner; and I arranged around the room boxes of various chemicals, and huge glass jars full of ill-smelling acids. In a junk-shop I found some antique astrological maps or charts covered with planets, moons, suns and comets, plentifully interspersed with demigods and demons. I also secured a stuffed alligator, and some dried skins of huge snakes and lizards. Altogether this half-subterranean chamber had a weird and ogreish look, sufficient to make the blood of the ordinary citizen, of an inquiring turn of mind, run cold in his veins. In addition to this, I purchased a large zinc vat, which was the only thing in the room meant for use and not for show. A lot of galvanic and electric instruments, with wires reaching in every direction, completed the imposing and impressive *tout ensemble.*

I assumed myself a grave and serious demeanor, and knitted my brows as if my brain were in the throes of profound thought; the processes of originality being, it is generally supposed, as laborious as the gestation of an elephant; while the truth is, a fertile mind breeds as rapidly and as easily as a rabbit.

I then hunted up a worker in metals, an intelligent man, and had him manufacture for me a large number of bars of iron, similar in size and shape to the bullion bars in which gold is shipped from California. I piled them up in my laboratory; and also laid in a supply of stout oaken boxes, with strong rope handles.

I was now ready for business.

I selected bars enough to make, as nearly as I could

judge, a million dollars' worth of gold; placed them in the zinc vat, covered them with a bath of cold water; made sure that all the doors and windows were carefully closed, and then drew the precious flask from my pocket. It really seemed to me that it shone with a bright light of its own, and the strange hieroglyphics which covered it, unlike any earthly alphabet I had ever seen, stood out with marvellous distinctness, as if the Golden Bottle rejoiced in the good work to humanity which it was about to accomplish, in turning those dead, black masses of iron into the means of liberating thousands of worthy people from wretchedness.

And then it occurred to me to try an experiment.

Were the wonderful results which the amber fluid in the flask accomplished due to any material and natural virtue, or were they simply the working of an extra-mundane, spiritual influence? And so to test the question I dropped but a single drop of the liquid into the tank, and instantly the water boiled and clouded, and the transformation took place. I then perceived that the Divine Power had no limitations as to quantity; and I could understand how, out of the coarse, unbolted oat-meal upon which he lived, the brain of Robert Burns could distil the sweetest lyrics in human speech, full of the divinest purity and most exquisite perfection. And, I said to myself, a few drops out of the golden flask of creative power, dropped into a human intellect, is sufficient to transform the thought, the literature, and the history of a people. I could have gone down on my knees before my precious treasure, and the God who stood behind it; but I kissed it and whispered to it: "You and I together shall yet redeem mankind from its bondage!"

The next day I packed my bars of bullion in some of the oak boxes with my own hands—still hard and strong from the rough work on that wretched Kansas farm, where I had toiled so long and so unprofitably—and an expressman carted the boxes to the mint.

CHAPTER X.

A MILLIONAIRE.

At the mint there was considerable hesitation and excitement. There was a great buzzing and putting together of heads, and applying of tests, and weighing and running to and fro, and summoning of experts, and scanning of myself with sidelong glances.

At length an elderly, gray-haired gentleman, with gold-rimmed spectacles on nose, looking like a compound of professor and mechanic, came to me, observing me keenly through his glasses the while, and said:

"May I ask your name, sir?"

"Ephraim Benezet," I replied.

"Of Kansas?"

"Yes."

"I thought as much," he replied.

"You find the gold all right?" I asked.

"Yes; the purest and finest we have ever received. Pardon me the question," he continued, after a pause, "but the bars do not have upon them any of the usual Californian or Australian or Montanian stamps and markings. May I ask where they come from?"

"I might reply," I said, "that that was my secret; but I will answer you frankly. I made them."

"You made them?" he exclaimed in great astonishment, while a crowd of the officers and employés gathered around us.

"Yes; I made them," I answered. "I have discovered the great secret which the alchemists of old sought in vain for a thousand years."

"It is most extraordinary," replied the old gentleman, thoughtfully. "Yesterday I should have said such a statement was the utterance of a lunatic; but there unquestionably is the gold, differing in some respects from any gold we have ever received, and yet gold of great fineness and purity. We have subjected it to all the tests known to science, and it has stood them all. The statutes of the government say that we must mint all gold bullion brought to us; it does not authorize us to inquire where it came from, or to question the antecedents of those who bring it. Our simple duty is to weigh the metal, issue our receipt therefore, and deliver over the coin to those who hold the receipt. I have made out the certificate. The gold you have brought amounts to $1,173,252.10. Here is your receipt. I congratulate you on your discovery, and on your great fortune realized and prospective; but I cannot but think that your discovery (and I have no reason to doubt your statement) is about to revolutionize the financial world from centre to circumference. When gold is as abundant as iron or lead, the occupation of this institution and others like it, all over the world, will be gone. With silver demonetized and gold as plentiful as brass, upon what will the business of the world rest? Pardon me, my dear sir; I have no right to intrude my reflections upon you, but I am an old man; I have spent nearly all my life in this building, which is literally a temple erected to the worship of gold; and now I see the god of my idolatry about to be overthrown forever. I feel like the highpriest of one of the ancient temples of the god Pan, when he beheld the great hall, sacred for thousands of years, empty and deserted; the worshippers all gone off in pursuit of the strange faith of the barefooted Nazarene. You have accomplished that which is about to overturn the world; we may still cry out 'Great is Diana of the Ephesians,' but the sceptre has departed from the yellow god from this hour."

The old gentleman's eyes grew moist. His faith in all things human was shaken, and he turned his back and walked sadly away. The other officials looked at me with reverent awe, as I folded up the precious slip of paper and quietly took my departure.

As I rode up Chestnut Street in my carriage, a vast sense of exultation came over me. I owned it all—houses, equipages, stores, goods, the people! The honor of man, the virtue of woman; the schools, colleges, churches; thoughts, opinions, beliefs; glory, fame, happiness, joy, suffering, everything—that little slip of paper was the title-deed of it all. I could buy up all the editors, professors, clergymen, critics, authors. In three months I could indoctrinate the world with the most pernicious or improbable beliefs;

I could have them taught in the schools; I could so fill the minds of the rising generation with them that mankind could not rid itself of them for a score of generations. "Gold! gold!" I cried; and then I repeated to myself the words of Timon:

"Thus much of this will make black, white; foul, fair;
Wrong, right; base, noble; old, young; coward, valiant.
               Why this
Will buy your priests and servants from your sides;
Pluck stout men's pillows from below their heads.
               This yellow slave
Will knit and break religions; bless the accursed;
Make the hoar leprosy adored: place thieves
And give them title, knee and approbation,
With senators on the bench: this it is
Will make the wappened widow wed again;
She whom the spital house and ulcerous sores
Would cast the gorge at."

I felt like one who has lighted a slow-match connected with a vast magazine of explosives, and draws back a space to witness the tremendous catastrophe, while the unconscious multitude pursue their avocations around him without the slightest anticipation of the uproar that is soon to shake the earth and fill the skies. I remembered that singular legend, that at the time of the birth of Christ, a mighty voice, tremendous and far-resounding, cried out, many times, in the darkness of the night, from the shores of the Mediterranean: "The great god, Pan, is dead! The great god, Pan, is dead!"

New things were coming apace upon the world. Old things must pass away. The "Golden Bottle" was a tremendous trust placed in my hands for the good of humanity.

I was an humble instrument in the hands of some incomprehensible, spiritual power, with benevolent purposes for the creature, man.

I need not describe my first deposit in the Commercial Bank—the rush of clerks and officers to look at me; the reverential and respectful greetings; the proffered services of the president; the awesome manner of the cashier; the inexpressible sense of power which came upon me as I reëntered my carriage.

I ordered $200,000 in cash sent at once to Archibald M. Hayes, of El Dorado, by express.

Twenty-five reporters called upon me that night. The afternoon papers were full of my visit to the mint. On the wings of the lightning the astounding intelligence spread to all parts of the civilized world. Scientists and empirics set to work everywhere, and the next few months men were driven crazy in Berlin, London, Paris, St. Petersburg, in vain endeavors to discover the same secret which had made me rich. The leading journals of the world were full of discussions of the probable consequences of such an extraordinary revelation upon the finances of the world. Every banker on the globe felt uneasy.

The gentlemen on the streets almost bowed their heads off; the women smiled so broadly that I could see their back teeth. People who would not have given ten cents to keep a blind beggar from starving to death, would have poured all they had in the world into my lap, simply because they knew I did not need it! Metaphorically speaking, the whole world was crawling in the mud all around me.

That night burglars, employed by scientists, broke into my laboratory and laboriously carried off a lot of acid worth about ten cents a gallon. They thought they had "the universal solvent."

The next day the papers were filled with nothing but—Ephraim Benezet! What an accomplished, learned, gracious, handsome gentleman I was! My very pictures were sublimated, until I looked like a cross between Jay Gould and Jove. Twenty photographers insisted I must sit to them. They wanted me in all sorts of poses and attitudes. I believe they would have taken me standing on my head, if I had been capable of assuming that position with any comfort to myself. The demand for my pictures, they assured me, was inexhaustible—the poorest men were the most eager to get them. They worshipped me in their dreams. I was to them the god of unlimited possibilities. A rain of invitations to dinners and suppers and clubs and entertainments fell upon me; the electric bell at the door was forever sounding with callers; the street swarmed with a vast mass of people who stood and stared and stared, as if the very bricks and mortar would reveal something of my marvellous secret.

I fled out of the back alley and rented a furnished house a mile away, under the name of John Jones, where I could enjoy some peace and quiet and escape from my greatness.

CHAPTER XI.

SOPHIE.

A DAY or two after the events detailed in the last chapter, I was quietly reading the morning paper, when I came across the following news item, in the telegraphic column from Omaha:

HORSEWHIPPED BY HIS MISTRESS.

Quite a scene was enacted to-day on Douglass Street. While the crowd of clerks and business men were hurrying to their dinners, about twelve o'clock, a tall, spare young woman darted out from a doorway, where she had been apparently waiting, and seized upon Mr. Charles Morrill, head of the well-known firm of Morrill, Browning, & Co., clothing manufacturers on Farnam Street, and horsewhipped him with a heavy whip such as teamsters use. Mr. Morrill struggled to release himself, but the girl's grip was like iron, and she applied the whip most energetically, until his face ran blood from the force of the blows. She was at last overpowered by two policemen and her victim liberated. She fought the officers like a wild-cat, but was eventually carried off to jail. Mr. Morrill was taken into the nearest drug store and his wounds dressed. He was interviewed by several newspaper reporters, but was very reluctant to talk. From a few words, however, which he dropped, it is inferred that he had held improper relations with the young woman for some time past, and that they had quarrelled because he would not accede to her extravagant demands for money. Mr. Morrill is a bachelor, and employs a great many women in his establishment, manufacturing clothing, and the prisoner was one of these. Her name is Sophia Hetherington; she came here a year or two ago from near El Dorado, Kansas, and has boarded for some time past at Mrs. Jenkins', No. 323 Summer Street. Mrs. Jenkins, when called upon, spoke in high terms of the girl, but of course she knew nothing of the improper relations between her and Mr. Morrill. Yesterday afternoon Sophia was brought before the Police Court and held for trial. Mr. Morrill appeared with his face almost covered by bandages, and testified to the assault, and the prisoner was held in eight hundred dollars bail to answer. Not being able to procure bail she was remanded to jail.

I was deeply moved as I read this telegram. "Poor Sophie," I said to myself, "you have fallen low, indeed!"

My heart went back to old times. I remembered Sophie when she was the brightest and handsomest girl in our neighborhood; the head of the spelling bees; the sweetest singer in the singing-school; the most graceful and daring horsewoman in Butler County; time and time again she had taken the prize at county fairs for horsemanship; the most untamed stallion became gentle as a lamb under her control. A picture of the fair girl rose before me—the tall, light, lissome figure; the large black eyes; the masses of dark hair; the bright, active, quick, energetic motions; the kindly smile. And I remembered certain sudden, unexpected looks which she had more than once darted at me, which gave me reason to believe that she loved me; and, for my part, my whole heart went out to her.

O poverty! poverty! Most dreadful and cruel doom and demon of humanity! You crushed out an industrious and noble family, and sent this poor girl to seek her fortune in the great city and find only ruin. Oh, may the curse of God fall on the plunderers of the people, who thus wreck homes and mangle lives, and drive angels swarming to the jaws of hell!

I loved Sophie. I love her still. She shall not remain friendless in that jail. Fallen though she may be, I will lift her out of her miseries, and give her a chance to earn an honest living; and to be once more all that she was before she wandered into the gates of that devouring metropolis. And who, after all, save God, shall judge the poor and the unfortunate? Who can measure, save their Maker, the awful stress of temptation put upon them before our pitiful human nature broke at its weakest point? God pity the women who fall! Womankind are the best and noblest of our race! Society and misgovernment are to blame for every woman who stumbles.

As soon as the cars would bear me I was in Omaha. My first step was to employ a lawyer. By depositing $800 as security, I obtained an order for Sophie's release. I ordered a carriage and drove to the jail. I exhibited the discharge and requested permission to see the prisoner. The jailer was very respectful; my fine clothes and the carriage insured that.

"Unlock the door," I said, in a whisper.

"Well, mister," said he in a low tone, "I wouldn't

advise you to go into that cell. That woman is a perfect tigress."

"Open the door," I replied, in the same low tone.

He did so. I looked in. A tall, spare figure was pacing rapidly up and down the narrow apartment. It wheeled around upon me and glared at me with great black eyes, as big as saucers; the countenance was thin and haggard, like the face of a tempest-beaten eagle. Her dress was plain and poor.

"What do you want?" she fiercely demanded. I saw she did not recognize me. Who could have recognized the farmer boy of Kansas in this stylishly-dressed gentleman?

"I come to you as a friend," I said quietly.

"I have no friends," she replied bitterly; "the poor are always friendless.

"I have gone upon your bail bond. The jailer here will tell you that you are free to leave this place at once. My carriage waits for you at the door."

"What pay do you expect for all this?" she demanded fiercely, with a sneer upon her lips.

"Nothing; but that you will answer me one question."

"What is that?"

"Are you guilty, as that man charges?"

"Guilty!" she fairly screamed, leaping from the floor in her rage, her energetic arms cleaving the air, "Guilty! Oh, the miscreant! the scoundrel! the impudent villain! I will kill him! I will kill him!

I will tear him to pieces with my bare hands in the open court!"

The jailer recoiled from the doorway in terror before this exhibition of tremendous rage.

"To think," she continued, "that a free American girl, because she would not yield to that wretch's lust, must be denied her wages, starved, and her good name taken from her, to force her into degradation. Oh, the infamous scoundrel! I should not have horsewhipped him; I should have sharpened a table-knife and driven it into his foul heart. To say I was his mistress, and demanded money from him! In these rags! Without food for twenty-four hours when I attacked him! Turned out of my boarding-house, because he held back the miserable pittance which I had earned by hard work, all to force me to his wishes. Oh! the damnable wretch! But he shall die, and I will gladly go to the gallows!"

I sprang forward and seized the energetic figure in my arms. She struggled and pushed me back, at arm's length, glaring at me fiercely, indignantly.

"Sophie!" I cried, "don't you know me?"

She looked at me intently.

"My God!" she cried, "it is Ephe."

The transformation that came over her was wonderful; the fire left her eyes; the drawn mouth softened; the very voice changed, and as I took her in my arms her figure relaxed, and she sobbed as if her heart would break; her whole frame shook in my embrace.

"Sophie," I said to her in a whisper, "your troubles are over. I have come here to marry you. All I wanted was to hear from your own lips that you were as pure as you were when we played together in dear old Kansas. We will never part again."

She held me at arm's length, gazing at me intently through her tears.

"But, Ephe," she said, "what does it all mean? You parted from me a poor farmer boy; you come here arrayed like a gentleman. I cannot understand it. Have my troubles turned my brain? Am I dreaming?"

"No, Sophie," I replied, "it is all real. I am indeed with you, and I am rich—rich beyond the wildest dream of the imagination—rich enough to buy up all Omaha, and all Nebraska. But come. Let us leave this dismal and wretched place."

She had no effects—nothing but the clothes she wore—everything else had been sold or pawned to buy food. But, penniless as she was, she was to me the richest possession in all the world—a true and noble woman, who loved me! I wouldn't have parted with her for Golconda. My treasure was restored to me pure and flawless. I was the happiest man in the world.

CHAPTER XII.

REVENGE.

In a little time we were married.

Sophie insisted on being properly apparelled, and a couple of days were consumed in purchases and dressmaking. The old, hard brand of poverty had been so burned into Sophie's soul, that I had to force her to buy articles befitting her new station in life; she was disposed to pinch and economize in most niggardly fashion. But I—I was proud of my bride, and the most costly jewels in the city, the most precious gifts, were not too good for her. I covered her with splendor, and when she stood up with me at the altar, the olive cheeks had begun to resume the softness of youth, the great eyes were tender with emotion, and no one could have recognized in the lithe and graceful and happy figure the woman who, but a little while before, had stormed and raved, in the stone cell of the county jail, like an enraged lioness. The whole town seemed to have turned out to witness the wedding, for the newspapers, as usual, had told everything; and it was known that "the gold-maker," the millionaire, the richest man in the world, had come from Philadelphia to Omaha to find a wife in the county prison. The glamour of my wealth at once spread over Sophie; the newspapers united in declaring that she was the most beautiful and spirited bride ever seen in Omaha; she, who had walked their streets for years in rags, unnoticed, with the pangs of hunger too often gnawing at her heart-strings. And every journalist in Omaha at once declared her innocent of all wrong-doing, and praised her for punishing with her own hand the slanderer of her honor.

But all this did not satisfy Sophie. She demanded justice upon Morrill; "Vengeance upon the wicked," she declared, "was the justice of God." My own disposition, I must own, is rather "easy-going." I argued with her that she had already sufficiently punished him. But no; the fiery advocate of right demanded that he be exposed and rendered harmless for the future.

What was I to do? What could I do as a good husband, but obey?

There was a detective agency in the city. Thither I wended my way, and employed a shrewd, taciturn fellow, named Brooks, to make some inquiries for me. He reported to me in a day or two that, while Morrill had the reputation of being wealthy, in his judgment he really was not; he had squandered his substance in profligacy; still his credit was good at the banks, and he and his firm owed a great deal of money. I gave him a lot of drafts, and told him to go ahead and buy up all the notes owed by Morrill and his firm that he could lay his hands on.

He called the next night and told me that he had made a startling discovery. In buying the notes held by one of the banks, he observed that the cashier was very particular to indorse them "without recourse" to the bank. This satisfied him that the bank had suspicions of some kind about the value of the paper, and did not desire to become responsible for it. The paper was indorsed by different prominent merchants of the city. Moved by curiosity, as much as anything else, Brooks selected a note for $10,000, with the name of the hardware firm of Snider & Co. on its back, and dropping into their office he casually inquired whether they were indorsers on any paper of Morrill, Browning & Co. Mr. Snider said yes, and, referring to a note-book, he said they had indorsed two notes for that firm, one of $3,000 and the other for $2,500.

"I have here a note for $10,000, indorsed by you," said Brooks.

"Let me look at it," said Mr. Snider. He examined it, and then held a whispered conversation with his chief clerk.

"We never indorsed that note," he said quietly.

"You mean to say that it is a forgery?"

"I mean to say that it was never indorsed by our firm."

"Whew!" said Brooks, and took his departure.

He went straight to police headquarters and had an officer appointed to "shadow" Morrill, and to arrest him if he tried to leave town. He then pursued his inquiries, and found two other notes that were forgeries. How much more forged paper Morrill & Co. still owed the banks he could not tell, but he thought it better to stop purchasing any more until he should receive further instructions from me. I thanked him for his energy and discretion.

While we were still speaking, another policeman called to see Brooks, and informed him that Morrill had been arrested at the depot, just as he was about to take the east-bound 10:20 night train, and was now at the police office.

I at once accompanied the officers thither. There I found Morrill, a chalky-faced, spongy-looking, youngish man, with a bald head, and no expression in his face but sensuality and low cunning. He was dressed in the height of the fashion; but I was pleased to notice certain livid markings on his face and neck, reminiscences of Sophie's whip. He was evidently a good deal disturbed, but was trying to bluster it out. A boon companion of his, a clerk in the establishment of Snider & Co., had given him, as we learned afterward, "a tip," and we had caught him just in time.

He was hectoring the lieutenant of police when we entered.

"What right have you," he said, "to arrest a prominent business man of Omaha, without a warrant, when he is attending to his own affairs. I will make every man pay who is at all concerned in this outrage."

Here he turned to Brooks and myself. The detective quietly took from his pocket three promissory notes, fastened together with a pin. A great change came over Morrill—he became very white and seemed to collapse; he recognized the notes.

There was a dead silence for a few minutes, then Brooks spoke:

"These signatures are forged. You know the penalty."

Morrill's features moved convulsively. Then he spoke as if his mouth was full of dust and the words would scarcely come:

"What do you want?"

"We want," said I, "to see you in the penitentiary, where you should have been long ago. A poor girl who had never committed a wrong in the world obtained work in your shop; you saw that she was innocent and beautiful; you laid siege to her virtue, and when she would not yield, you kept back, under lying pretences, the poor pittance of wages you owed her, to starve her into submission; and this was an American girl, with better blood in her veins than you possess, for her ancestors had fought in every great battle for liberty ever waged on this continent; and not content with all this, you were unutterably base enough to tell the world that this pure and innocent girl had been your mistress, and by thus branding her, you sought to force her down the steps of sin into death and hell. You are an unspeakable villain. But we have the proofs of your guilt here, and

I am that young lady's husband, and it is my mission to see that you receive your just deserts."

The craven wretch fell on his knees and prayed for mercy. He had, he said, money enough with him to pay those three notes, about $27,000. He would give it to me if I would allow him to take the midnight train.

His tears moved my pity. He saw it and pleaded with increased fervor.

He would, he said, sign a statement completely admitting that his charges against my wife were absolute lies. Call in a magistrate. He would swear to it. He would do anything—only let him escape.

I wrote a letter to Sophie, telling her everything, and sent it by a messenger. He returned in a little while, with her answer, written in her large, bold hand, at the end of my communication:

"I want neither his money nor his exculpation. Let justice take its course."

The miserable wretch fairly shrieked as I read this reply to him.

I signed the necessary complaint and withdrew.

The next day it was known that the great house of Morrill, Browning & Co. had failed, and that the head of the firm was in prison, held under a dozen different charges of forgery.

When the sewing-girls heard of the failure of the firm, and came hurrying for the little sums due them, and which yet, little as they were, represented bread, shelter, and life, Brooks, the detective, met them on the front steps of the closed establishment, and sent them for their pay to a certain room of our hotel. There they found their old companion, Sophie, who welcomed them with kind and encouraging words, and seated them at a banquet, such as they might have dreamed of in their dreams, but never had enjoyed in fact; and Sophie, at the head of the table, after giving to each one a liberal sum of money, amply sufficient for present needs, got up and made them a speech. Brooks and I hid behind the half-opened folding doors, and heard every word of it. She said:

"Girls, you have all heard of my good fortune. A little while ago, and I was as poor as the poorest of you—poorer, for I was in prison, and I did not think I had a friend in the world, and I had not a hope in all the world except that I might kill that villain Morrill and be hung for it. Well, girls, I am now the wife of the richest man in the world, and what is more, the best and kindest-hearted man on the globe; for he came all the way from Philadelphia to Omaha to take me out of a prison and cover me with diamonds and marry me; yes, when every newspaper in Omaha said I was a prostitute! And I tell you, girls, I would die for that man, and so would every one of you, if she had a such husband. [Here some of the girls applauded, but more of them wept; Brooks and I could hear their sobs.]

"But I want you to understand," Sophie continued, "that if luck has lifted me up I don't intend to forget those that are down. [Cheers.] I am just as much your sister now as I was when I skimped and pinched and toiled, morning, noon and night, to continue an honest girl, and not be forced out under the gas-lamps on the street, hunting for reprobates. [Great clapping of hands.] I am going to talk it over with Ephe—I mean Mr. Benezet—and get him to advise me what is the best way to help you, for I know you don't want to be beggars, living on the bounty of even an old friend; you want a chance to earn an honest living, and get a fair day's wage for a fair day's work. [Cheers and cries of "That's so."] And I don't mean to help only you girls that used to work with me for Morrill, Browning & Co., and be jewed down by old Browning, and winked at by Morrill, and cheated in all kinds of ways until our hearts were as bitter as death; no, I am going to help every poor, struggling girl in Omaha, and if Ephe— I mean Mr. Benezet—stands by me, every girl in *all the world*, and if he don't stand by me, much as I love him, I won't live with him. There!"

I lifted my hand to wipe away some curious liquid things that came out of my eyes on my cheeks, and stood still there; and as I did so I heard Brooks sniffle, and, when I turned to look at him, I'll be hanged if that detective wasn't crying. My heart warmed to him that minute, and I engaged him on the spot to give up his place and work for me for five years, at a royal salary.

But Sophie was still speechifying.

"I tell you girls," she said, "we will begin right

now. We will organize ourselves into a committee. I am chairwoman. I appoint Mary McLeod treasurer, and Susan Dunning secretary; and each of you is a committee of one to hunt up the wretched and bring them to those two girls, our officers; and I will furnish them the money to relieve their pressing necessities, until we get our grand reformation started. And, girls, don't go inquiring too closely into any woman's past history, provided she wants to do right. Why, girls, it is the most pitiful thing in the world to think that those whom Nature has made weakest, most dependent, most defenceless, should have the whole weight of a universe of temptations and necessities piled on them to crush them; and it is the most shameful thing in all the world that when they fall under their burden, not only vicious men but virtuous women unite to keep them from ever rising again. Why, girls, the strong, warm instinct of love, without which a woman is not a woman, becomes the very engine of destruction to her who has most of it. Of course, if a girl is bad by choice, you want nothing to do with her; for it is God's rule that the race should be preserved at its best; but open all the doors, set back the lintels, tear down the whole front of the house, for those who want to come back to goodness; pass a sponge over their weak past and point them forward to a strong future."

A happier set of poorly-clad, chattering girls never streamed down a hotel's stairs than that crowd, when Sophie dismissed them. Ah! those were busy days.

My wife sat in perpetual session, with an unending string of callers, and my money flowed out like water. But what did I care? I would have fed the whole world to please Sophie, and Sophie was as happy as the day was long.

CHAPTER XIII.

SOPHIE'S PLAN.

WE were at breakfast in our own room.

"Ephe," said Sophie, "I have been thinking a great deal lately as to how I can help the laboring classes, especially the women."

"Yes, my dear," I said, "and what conclusions have you reached?"

"I have been thinking," she said, "that mankind is not naturally bad. In fact, they have a real sympathy with goodness and truth. Men do wrong through the pressure of society, in the struggle to live. I remember reading a French story of a lot of galley-slaves, who had conspired to murder one of their number, and while waiting for an opportunity to strike the deadly blow, one of them commenced to tell a pitiful story he had heard, of cruelty and injustice done to a boy, and the very assassins wept over the romance; they would have risked their lives to defend that poor, persecuted boy, and yet they were the basest of mankind, and at that very time contriving to do a murder."

"Well," I asked, "how do you apply that general conclusion?"

"In this way:—Morrill, Browning & Co, did not give us better wages because if they had other firms would have undersold them, and they would have been driven out of business. And if all the Omaha manufacturers of clothing had met together and agreed to raise prices for work, then New York and Chicago and Philadelphia would have rushed their goods in at lower prices and closed them out. And if they got all the American cities to put up wages, still Europe would put them down. And if all the manufacturers in the world united to pay their employés better compensation, the workmen would still hold their advantages at the mercy of any man more cruel or greedy than the rest who would reduce prices, and then all the rest would have to tumble to the same level."

"Well," I said, "that is plain enough; but what remedy have you devised?"

"It seems to me evident, therefore," continued Sophie, "that the remedy cannot come from the employers of labor. No matter how just or kindly they may be, individually, they are in the grasp of a relentless necessity; they *must* crowd wages down to the lowest level at which the laborers can live. The remedy must come, therefore, from the laborers, by thorough organization for self-defence, and by asserting the dignity of their calling at the ballot-box; by insisting upon a share in the government, and turning its forces to lift up and defend their class. But the sewing-women are so weak, so helpless, so poor, and sin opens so many gilded doors of temptation all around them; and it is so easy to slip into wickedness, that it seems to me relief must come outside of the ranks of their employers or themselves."

"Admirably reasoned," I said, very proud of my able wife, "but your argument leads you right up against a stone wall of helplessness."

"No," she replied, "you forget my first proposition, that mankind is naturally good and generous and sympathetic. If it were not for that this would be indeed a *beast* world, as hopeless and wicked as Dante's Inferno. In that God-implanted instinct of goodness lies the hope of mankind. Now suppose we organize a society of women — women of wealth, women of the middle classes, to rescue and save and lift up their unfortunate sisters, the honest toilers, by agreeing to purchase only those goods that were made by the women themselves, without the intervention of middlemen. If the women were roused to action they would very soon convert their husbands—you know how it is in this family," she added, laughing; and I subscribed to my subjugation by getting right up and kissing her; without the slightest impulse, on my part, to resist the outrageous domination of which I was the victim.

"Well," she continued, "as soon as we got the women ready to stand by us, we would open stores or repositories where the goods made by the women would be sold directly to the consumers, and the money which now goes to make a few families of middlemen very rich, would go to make thousands of poor families happy."

"I like that idea," I said, "it seems practicable. How had we better begin?"

"I think," she answered, "I will get you to give a banquet to all the editorial fraternity of Omaha, and explain our ideas and ask them to help us."

"Oh no!" I replied, "that wouldn't do. The American newspapers have no sympathy with the people, and will do nothing to help them."

"I think you are wrong there," she replied; "where certain interests own the stock of a great journal of course the editors, like lawyers, have to defend the side they depend on for their bread and butter. But the editors are men like yourself; and many of them are very good men; and, as I told you, goodness is natural to all men, and evil is artificial and represents simply the pressure of necessity. The average editor wants to be as near right as the circumstances of his position will permit; and he represents a tremendous power for good or evil; and if he don't work for truth he will work for error."

"Well, my dear," I said, "I will follow your advice; I will give the editors a banquet."

And a grand banquet it was—no expense was spared; every one came that was invited; for all were curious to see more of the man and his wife whom all the newspapers, and all the people, were talking about; the new Count of Monte Cristo, the modern Crœsus, the Paracelsus, the "gold-maker."

After the viands were cleared away, I made them a speech and explained our purposes. As soon as they learned that what I proposed had nothing to do with free silver, or national banks, or tariff, or watered stock of railroads, or anything else concerning which they were tied up neck-and-heels by their stockholders; that, in short, it was a mere work of humanity, for the benefit of women, they entered heartily into the scheme, and promised the full influence of their several journals in its favor. In fact a pleasanter or kindlier set of gentlemen I had not met with for a long time, and we parted with expressions of mutual good will and esteem.

CHAPTER XIV.

THE MEETING.

The newspapers had performed their part nobly. The house was packed from pit to dome. Three-fourths of the audience were ladies. The first families were all present. That was a hopeful sign; for society, unlike religion, moves from the top downwards. Every working-woman was also present, arrayed in her poor best.

First there was some grand music.

Then the mayor of the city introduced me. I had a rapturous reception; my popularity, I think, principally depended on the fact that I had married Sophie. But every opera-glass was levelled to inspect the man who had made the most wonderful discovery of the age. There was profound silence as I began.

"Ladies and gentlemen," I said, "we are here to inaugurate to-night, with your help, a great work of philanthropy. We are here to take steps to secure better wages to the working-women of Omaha, the women who work in shops and factories. I know that in such a work we will have your sympathy and support. [Cheers.] We propose to organize a society every member of which will pledge herself or himself to buy only the articles manufactured by women, directly of the women themselves, in stores which I shall establish, so that whatever value their labor has added to the articles in question will go directly to themselves, the women. In this way their wages will be largely increased, and they will live better and be happier. You will get the goods you purchase at the same price you pay now; the only difference will be that all the profits of the labor of thousands of workers will not be absorbed, as it is now, by a score or so of middlemen. The working-women having better wages will be able to buy more of the merchants, more clothes, more food, etc.; they will be able to pay better rent for better homes. Every one in Omaha will have a resulting share in their prosperity, and you will do a great and good work, and help your city without it costing you a single dollar which you would not spend under existing conditions.

"But, ladies and gentlemen, you will perceive that I am no orator; I shall therefore introduce to you my wife, who has conceived this work of charity, and who can best explain it to you."

And with this demure and practical statement of the objects of the meeting, I stepped to the wings, and led Sophie forward.

Lord! I thought they would take the roof off the house! The whole audience was white with waving handkerchiefs; the men flung a shower of hats and caps into the air, and such a roar went up as if Niagara had just broken in at the front door. The sewing-girls stood up on the benches and screamed themselves hoarse, and it was a good five minutes before quiet was restored.

And a very pretty picture Sophie made, standing there all in black, without an ornament save a single rose in her hair, her face smiling and her eyes dancing. Ah! I had married a wonderful woman without knowing it. She was a marvellous orator. There was an electric instantaneousness about her movements I never saw in any other speaker. With the ordinary person it takes some time to convey the emotions from the brain to the arms; and hence the action lags away behind the thought, like a caboose at the end of a lengthy freight train. But with Sophie the moment the thought struck your intelligence the hand went out and typified it. And when she was excited she thought in metaphors, tropes, parables, and figures. But behind the mind was a glorious character, and behind both a transcendent purpose. Oh, it was a glory to listen to her—nay, you did not listen, you instantaneously understood; your mind moved with hers, as if the ordinary channels of hearing were suspended, and a divine telepathy welded the audience to the speaker.

"Sisters," she began, ignoring the men as not worthy of her attention; "Sisters, I· want to talk straight at your hearts, right into your souls.

"Part of you are mothers. You have fair and

lovely sons. Some of them are rocking in the cradle; some are playing in the nursery; some have the down of adolescence just blooming on their cheeks. You love them! Oh, how dearly you love them! You have studied every fold of flesh of their bodies; through the crystal windows you have looked down deep into their souls, and beheld the pellucid innocence dwelling within them. Every bit of them, from the flossy hair to the little pink toes, is precious to you, bone of your bone, flesh of your flesh. How often have they slept in your arms while you dreamed dreams of their coming greatness and goodness. The sound of their prattle, the ripple of their laughter is sweeter in your ears than all the music of all the world. You send them out with springing steps and bright eyes to walk the pathways of life. They go with the hot and bounding blood of youth beating in their veins. Look down yonder gayly lighted street. There walks your beloved—your pride—your hope. And who is this bright creature who approaches him, who stops him. It is a woman, driven by hunger to hunt for prey. She comes to him as Eve came to Adam—a beautiful and brilliant temptation. Every inherited trait of countless generations of men tugs at the poor boy's heart. She leads him away. 'Her feet go down to death; her steps take hold on hell.' Your boy is destroyed. He dies not, but he lives debased, diseased, disgraced. Your tears are hot and wet upon your face. 'I will go forth,' you say, 'and slay that monster—that devourer of the innocent and the beautiful; that murderer of the hopes of mothers; that trampler on the hearts of women.'

"Stop, sister! Who set that monster to hunt your son? Who drove her from honest industry to such a dreadful career?

"It was *you*—yes, YOU! Why the mockery of these tears? You are more to blame than the temptress. For you were rich and intelligent and influential, and you stood by and saw that poor, weak girl driven to the most hideous of all alternatives—starvation or shame. *You* did it! *You* have sacrificed your child! *You* nursed the wild beasts that have devoured him. *You* have driven the dagger into your own heart.

"Listen to the story of that girl who has poisoned your son's flesh and life, and left him a living wreck on the doorstep of your fair mansion.

"I see a farm-house in wide fields; a man ploughing; a woman at her household duties; several children playing, with rude toys, upon the floor. Look at this little flaxen-haired girl, pretty as a dream, innocent as the angels in heaven. It is the home of industry and poverty. The sun, as he appears above the eastern horizon, finds them at work, and when he sinks in the far west they are still toiling. *What*, you say, cannot all these vast fertile fields, with their huge crops of food, feed these half-dozen people? Ah, they do not work for themselves. They are the bond-slaves of others. Cunning customs and laws and practices enchain them with invisible shackles;

men who live far away—whom they know not—whom they never saw nor will ever see,—take their earnings. Like Sisyphus they roll the great rock of toil up the hill of endeavor, and ever and anon, as it nears the top, it thunders back upon them, and they weep, for industry is in vain! By an old-world superstition money, a thing intended to simply measure values, a yard-stick, a scale—is made to breed money, faster than the earth can breed crops.

"At last there comes a dismal day. The father is dead—crushed under the rolling rock, the Sisyphine weight of interests, of taxes, of monopolized markets, of cruel trusts, of every form of human selfishness and cunning. The little family is scattered. The small flaxen-haired beauty, whom we saw playing with the rag doll, is now grown into budding womanhood; she should have become the mother of a sturdy race of country-bred boys and girls; of boys as manly and girls as fair as your own; for she had in her veins the blood of the best races of men in all this world. But she never knows home, or love, or motherhood—sacred motherhood. Driven from the open country, where all the lands are concentrating in the hands of the few, she has gone to swell the turbid and turbulent stream of the muddy multitude in this great wicked city. She toils, she is weak; health fails, starvation stares her in the face; she falls into sin, she becomes a merciless hunter of men, armed with the poisoned darts of disease and death; your sweet-faced boy encounters her; he is gone, lost, wrecked, ruined. She has revenged her wrongs on the innocent; she has stricken down your best-beloved.

"O sister, think of it! What wages did that poor girl work for before she fell? Ask her employer. Look with astonishment at the meagre prices which represented almost continuous labor in a garret, with insufficient food. Her toil went to enrich her employer. Her life was worn out for naught.

"Would you, O sister woman, I put it boldly to you—would *you* have resisted leering, gilded temptation, with nothing before you but a hopeless life of such wretchedness? Is it a wonder that many fall? Is it not rather a wonder that any stand? By your sinful indifference you have filled the streets with temptations; you have opened wide the gates of hell; you have set a large part of the human race to preying on the remainder. They cannot help it. They *must* do it or *starve!*

"And look you! I have talked to you about your son. But who is it sits beside you? Your husband; the beloved of your heart. Does he not hourly walk through the ambush of swarming temptations? How long can *he* stand? Go ask the divorce courts! Go read the catalogue of wrecked homes, of blighted firesides, of divided families.

"O sisters! This is one of the crying evils of our day—the root of innumerable miseries, the fountain-head of incalculable sufferings.

"'For she hath cast down many wounded; yea, many strong men have been slain by her.

"'Her house is the way to hell, going down to the chambers of death.'

"Can you cure this evil? Yes.

"Women are, as a rule, naturally good. They do not fall into debasement and defoulment willingly. Withdraw the dreadful and crushing strain now resting upon the sex. Give them a just and fair return for their toil, and they will no longer carry desolation and death into your household.

"Women, wives, mothers—help us in this great work! It is *your* work. Agree with us never again to purchase any product of woman's labor where the woman does not receive the full price of the same, less a small percentage paid to other women to sell it.

"Save your homes, save your children, save humanity.

"Are you ready to go with us? Are you ready to sign?"

There was a thunderous "aye, aye," and great cheering; and instantly a hundred sewing-girls darted down the aisles with printed forms of a pledge, and it seemed to me that nearly every one in that great house signed the papers. Then they were carried up and laid in a pile on the platform, and again the enthusiasm broke forth in thunders of applause. Then committees were appointed to establish branch societies in every ward, and the greatest meeting ever held in Omaha adjourned amid immense enthusiasm.

The next day stores were hired in different parts of the city, and signs put up: "WOMEN'S COÖPERative Association;" and soon hundreds of women were at work, making all manner of goods, while steady streams of purchasers flowed in from morning until night.

And then Sophie started the erection of great buildings in different parts of the town, after plans of her own: ten, fifteen stories high. The lower floors were used as stores, the upper as bed-rooms and work-rooms for the girls. On each floor there was a kitchen to cook the food, and shops to sell, at a trifle more than first cost, the articles of all kinds which they needed to buy. The topmost floor of all contained reading-rooms, libraries, music-rooms and a great apartment for balls and public meetings. Here twice a week there was dancing, and the other nights instructive lectures, with preaching by the most distinguished clergymen on Sundays, day and night.

What a happy set of girls they were! Their wages were doubled, quadrupled, their expenses reduced, their lives happy. Everything that was best in them was called to the surface; whatever was evil was forced downward and disappeared. The angels of heaven, if submitted to earthly conditions of pain and want and suffering, would soon become demons. Crime is simply the output of pressure; a testimony to the wickedness of man's laws, now or in the past. The women had charge of the whole business. They appointed committees who looked after everything; supervised the stores, examined the books, saw that purchases were made at cost, and that no cunning fellow inserted a steal between them and their necessities. The institutions were soon in a self-sustaining condition. It was a sort of practical communism, but one not ignoring independent individualism. One fire warmed many hundreds, the same engine worked a multitude of sewing-machines, the same music delighted thousands, the same cooking apparatus prepared the food for hundreds. A few capable women were paid to overlook the whole establishment; to see that cleanliness prevailed everywhere; that order and propriety were enforced. The appearance of the girls improved wonderfully. Their faces filled out, their cheeks had the glow of health, their clothes were vastly better; they had all the look of cultured and wealthy ladies; their very bearing showed independence, safety, and happiness. No longer insulted by the brutal male underlings who had formerly to pass upon their work, their manners and speech became courteous, for every woman instinctively desires to be a lady. These establishments were little paradises on earth. Night-schools were established in them to educate those who could not read and write; art-schools for those who desired to rise to higher pursuits; and the various professions proper for women, as typesetting, typewriting, stenography, bookkeeping, etc., were taught to those who intended to follow those pursuits. Male visitors were permitted to visit them in the drawing-rooms and at the balls in the presence of the superintendents, after they had established that they were honorable men of good reputation. And even the rudest of these visitors soon perceived that there had taken place an elevation of character and bearing upon the part of the young women; they were no longer abject, dependent, dejected, necessitous; they were ladies in the full sense of the word. Many were sought in marriage, as an improved type of womankind.

My wife insisted, with a broad charity, upon one condition: no woman who engaged a room or bed in any of these establishments was ever asked to give any account of her previous history. It was sufficient that applicants should be moral, industrious and lady-like in their conduct after they entered the institution. No girl was permitted to assail another about any part of her past career, should she have knowledge of anything discreditable to her. The result was that in a little time the news of this great reformation spread into thousands of obscure and disgraceful places, and, day by day, those who had been driven to sin by suffering and wretchedness disappeared from their accustomed haunts and entered upon happy lives of prosperous virtue; and so delightful to them became the new respectability, and the society of good women, that no temptation could have drawn them back to their old courses. The hunters of men disappeared from the streets, and the houses of sin had to be replenished from other cities, where still able and intelligent merchants, leading citizens, were engaged in the noble work of crushing women into wretchedness and crime.

Sophie was delighted. She was "as busy as a nailer." The people of the city were very much pleased. They swarmed in great multitudes to the evening lectures, and the balls, and the Sunday services, to look at the well-dressed, handsome, happy women; and to think that all this wonderful transformation *had not cost them, or any one else except the former employers, the loss of a single penny.* There was the wonder! A mighty charity that was no charity! And then Sophie established a national society, and sent out speakers and organizers north, south, east, and west, to agitate for the new movement, and open stores and erect institutions all over the country. The newspapers of other cities took it up, and a great wave of humanitarianism and tenderness to womanhood spread far and wide, from the Atlantic to the Pacific coast; and good men and women were found everywhere who stood ready to carry forward the mighty reform, until every woman in the land was in the "Woman's League of America," pledged to buy no goods made by women except from the women themselves. It was a simple creed, but it worked wonders. And the habitations of evil became almost tenantless; no longer were wretched creatures driven by hunger to clutch at men on the public streets, and offer them disease in exchange for bread. The race rose with the elevation of the *matrix* of the race; for the river of humanity cannot ascend above the level of its fountain—woman.

And oh, the incalculable happiness that burst from this source, wide expanding as the rays of the rising sun!

Hunger—direst foe of everything that lives—no longer ate like a canker at the vitals of delicate women. No longer cold assailed them, as they sat by their scarcely-heated stoves, balancing in doubt between the pain of freezing and the cost of the invaluable "black diamonds." No longer were all womanly wants and desires, hopes and aspirations suppressed.

The very working-men rejoiced in the good work, for in the degradation of women they had found the great leveller of their own wages; the poor creatures had to underbid them in the market of toil or starve. Their sisters had been their enemies—their daughters their destroyers.

And to the women it seemed as if God had indeed entered into the world and driven the devil back to his den. The earth became beautiful, peaceful, happy, hopeful; full of all kindness and goodness. And tender feelings of love grew up between the poor workers and the rich ladies; they were once more flesh of one flesh, and sisters of one blood; walking hand in hand, behind Him of Nazareth; and every step they took together joy and love sprang up under their feet, and the earth became more beautiful. And rich women, who had been idle and useless, and had frittered away their lives in the competition of shallow vanities, and the empty chit-chat which go to make up their daily conversations, about the weather and the fashions and their servants, found something ennobling to do, something to drive away their *ennui*, something that they felt all divine powers, outside and inside the visible world, could approve: the elevation of their sisters, and in it the protection of their children. And they entered heart and soul into the great reform. They formed societies, they contributed money, they became enthusiastic; and so effectively did they work that it almost seemed that there would soon be found no degraded women in all this nation, save such poor, oppressed creatures as were forced out from across the sea, from those horrible lands of injustice, oppression, and cruelty.

And so an endless work was begun which was destined to transform the human race. *Not charity, but justice.* Not stealing from the poor and giving them back part of it, with many airs and flourishes and ostentations; but stopping the stealing, and *permitting industry to keep the fruits of its own toil.* How beautiful is industry when it means plenty, prosperity, happiness, a clear mind, a serene heart, a comfortable home! How horrible is industry when it means grinding and unrequited toil—toil that does not afford fuel to keep up the fires under the engine that does the work of life; toil that enriches not the toiler, but the idle stranger! Is it any wonder that under such conditions the soul of the laborer becomes bitterer than death and blacker than hell, and he is ready to curse God and die; aye, ready to blow up a world that permits such things without protest?

Of course I am anticipating events which required weeks and months and years to carry out. I resume the thread of my narrative.

CHAPTER XV.

I HEAR FROM KANSAS.

We returned to Philadelphia. All Omaha grieved when we took our departure. The poor girl who had horsewhipped her persecutor had become a queen among women. Her popularity was unbounded. I was quite dwarfed beside her, and yet I rejoiced in my inferiority; for I was only able to reach the minds of men, but she possessed that subtle, unconscious, occult art which ties a million hearts to one heart. We have built up innumerable schools, properly enough, to educate the minds of the race, but the soul, the sympathies outride them all. "One touch of nature makes the whole world kin." There are great *influences* which cannot be tabulated, which do not appear in your census-tables, with the wheat, the pork, the corn, the dollars, the bonds, but which yet, in the affairs of this world, count for more than all these things put together. They touch, as it were, the *female* side of the universal nature; men do not *think* them, they *feel* them; and when they move through the consciences of a race, they overwhelm nations and overthrow dynasties.

When I reached Philadelphia, I asked my servant

for my mail. In Kansas, in my obscure days, I had received about one letter a month; my correspondence had increased greatly since I became famous. But I was not prepared for the sight which met my eyes, as my man, with a smile, led me into another room, where I found a lot of sacks piled up several feet high, every sack full of letters.

I employed a dozen clerks to read, separate, and tabulate them. Three-fourths were applications for help; some were suggestions of new inventions; others offers of services; some were from knaves or lunatics, demanding large sums as the price of my life, and still others were invitations to invest capital in different enterprises, from building railroads to manufacturing toothpicks.

I directed my detective, Brooks, who had accompanied me, to select assistants and inquire into every case where application was made for charity, and to relieve those he thought deserved help.

Among the letters was one from my mother, and another from my father. My mother's letter was as follows:

DEAR EPHRAIM:—I take my pen in hand to let you know that we are all enjoying good health, thanks be to the Dispenser of all goodness, and I hope this will find you the same.

Our old cow, Blossom, had a steer calf yesterday. I have a great deal of trouble with the chickens. I fear a skunk gets into the coop at night. I have lost three lately. one of them was that pretty brown hen with the top-knot; you remember her; he is very poor, and has a hard time to get along with his big family. Mrs. Smithers was telling me yesterday that she didn't really know what they would do for the mortgage; it is due next month, and the congregation is so poor that he cannot collect anything scarcely whatever. Father has made a number of improvements on the farm. He has built a new barn with a windmill, and a new paling fence around it; and bought a new team and another carriage, and the farm that joins us on the west, that the Hetheringtons used to own: you remember Sophy—a good girl Sophy was. But your father is a changed man: he is lending out money on chattel-mortgages at five per cent a month. He is greedy to make all he can, and has left the Alliance. I tell him that at his time of life; his thoughts should be on another and a better world; but it's no use talking to him, and he wants to buy all the land that joins him. The money you have loaned out all over the county has helped a great many poor people, and I hope God will bless you for it.

Your loving mother,
Matilda D. Benezet.

I made out from this mixed letter that the Rev. Mr. Smithers, a good, worthy man, who was living in a little house, on a town lot in El Dorado, was embarassed, and that success had transformed my good father from a philanthropic member of the Farmers' Alliance into a grasping money-lender. There was no chance, in consequence of my loans through Mr. Hayes, for him to get big rates on farm mortgages, and so he was lending money at high figures on chattel mortgages.

I wrote to my mother as follows:

My dear Mother:—I am glad to receive your letter, and to learn that you are all well. I know that you are a good, kind, charitable woman, always anxious to help some poor person in trouble, or to nurse some one who is sick. You have not asked me for any money, but I know you can use it to advantage; and so I inclose you a draft for ten thousand dollars. Put it in bank and draw against it as you want it. Pay off Mr. Smithers' mortgage, and give him as much more as will help him out of his troubles. If there are any other clergymen who will accept help from you be sure to give it to them. Don't make any distinction as to denominational differences. The ministers are all useful men, and all, working together for the good of man, acccording to their best lights; and I have an idea that, so far as belief is concerned, all roads lead to heaven, whether they be the wide and beaten highways of authority, or the mountain goat-paths of honest, individual judgment. The Kingdom of Heaven is not fenced in, even with a barbed-wire fence; but is as open as God's mercy and as extensive as His goodness.

Don't fail to call upon me for more money when you spend that which I send. Remember it costs me nothing, and one can afford to be charitable under such circumstances. So don't let any one around you suffer. Affectionately your son,

EPHRAIM.

And then I read my father's letter. It was as follows:

DEAR EPHE:—I saw Mr. Hayes the other day. He said that some one had told you that I was ready, the night you left El Dorado, to help the bankers arrest you as a lunatic, for lending out money at two per cent a year. There isn't a word of truth in that story. I wonder how men can tell such lies. Deacon Jones and Mr. Smith, the bankers, came out to see me that afternoon, and told me that you were going to let every man in the county have money at two per cent a year; and that it would ruin all the business of the county, and drive our best men away; and they thought you were crazy as a bed-bug. And I said that no man in his senses would lend money for that rate, when he could just as easy get twenty-four per cent to forty per cent; and that I would go into town the next day and see about it. And that was all there was to that yarn. And I went in the next day, and they were going to arrest you, and they couldn't find you; and I would like to know how you got off. But I must say, as your father, that I think it is a shame to lend money at that rate. Why, it has driven all our bankers out of the county except Mr. Smith, and he is closing up his business to go too. It has just ruined the mortgage business. I offered money at ten per cent on farm mortgages, and couldn't get a taker: I will have to go into the next counties; and I can't get any interest on my money except on chattel mortgages, and your two per cent folly is ruining even that business, for people are getting out of debt. In fact, I begin to wonder what the capitalistic class is to do in this county. They will have to quit, or go to work. And I want to say, my dear Ephe, that all that talk we used to listen to, at the Alliance, about the Plutocrats and the sufferings of the farmers, is a lot of "rot." The farmers are to blame for their condition; they are much better off than the same class is in Europe. I know I used to swallow that stuff and believed in it, but I have got my eyes open. The farmers should work harder and live more economically, and they wouldn't be in debt. Look at the way they leave their machinery standing out, when they should put it under cover. To tell the truth, I have very little sympathy with such men. There must be distinctions in society—the Declaration of Independence is all wrong—all men are not created equal; there must be a richer and a poorer class; and some must work for the benefit of others of more intelligence. I hope this two per cent a year business does not mean that you are going to join the anarchistic and communistic crowd of cranks and lunatics who are trying to interfere with the laws of nature and the great "law of supply and demand."

As there is scarcely anything to do in this county, I think of starting a bank in the city of Topeka; and I want you to send me fifty thousand dollars, or you might make it one hundred thousand dollars, for it costs you nothing; and I will so use the money as to leave an estate worth something to the family when I die, and you will have your share of it.

Your affectionate father,

JOHN BENEZET.

I did not know whether to be amused or angered by this epistle of my worthy sire; and so I sat down and wrote him the following reply:

My dear Old Shylock:—I have just received your letter. You are a pretty one! A little success has turned your shallow old head, as it has the heads of thousands before you. The devil of insatiate greed has entered into your heart, and you have become an oppressor and plunderer of your fellow-men. I am sorry I ever gave you a penny, for you have done harm with it, and not good; and I shall not send you a dollar, save what may be necessary for your personal expenses. And, like a wretched old poll-parrot, you repeat the stale lies and excuses for cruelty and injustice which you have picked up from the small storekeepers and the still smaller money-lenders of the village. You ought to be ashamed of yourself. "The farmers should work harder and live more economically!" Don't you know, from your own experience, that they work twice as hard and live twice as poorly as the people of the villages? Who is it talks this kind of stuff? The middlemen, who sit in easy chairs, doing nothing, while the farmers walk through the mud between the plough-handles, from morning until night, with about ten pounds of clay sticking to each foot; or toil at the threshing-machine or on the straw-stacks, with the sweat running in streams from their dust-begrimed faces, while their *masters* of the towns smoke their cigars and read the daily papers, or the last new novel, and talk about the lazy farmers. "Live more economically!" Why, the inhabitants of the cities consume ten dollars of luxuries where the farmer consumes one. The board bill of the merchant for a week would support a farmer and all his family for a month. Where do you find the empty oyster cans and the mutton-chop bones? Is it around the back doors of the farmer's houses? No; pork fat and baked beans, with molasses, is their highest conception of luxury. And yet, who are best entitled to the good things of this life; the men who create all wealth, or the men who appropriate it? And then you utter the same old "chestnut" about leaving machinery out-of-doors. I repeat, I am ashamed of you. Do you remember the old reaper that stood all last year behind the barn. Why didn't you build a shed over it? Simply because you hadn't the money to buy the lumber; and you had no credit, and nothing left to morgtage for security for the lumber. But it might be said you could have made a thatched shed with straw and a few poles. True, but even the poles, in a prairie country, cost money; and you were utterly demoralized and despairing. You can't make a man work without hope. All the faculties you had were concentrated on the question of when you would be kicked off the farm, and what you would do next. And you have gone back on the Alliance! Of course you have. You have joined the great army of capitalists, and the workers are now your slaves and foes. It is to me the most astonishing thing in nature that the small tradesmen, whose own prosperity must depend entirely upon the prosperity of the farmers, fight every effort of the producing classes to improve their condition. They seem to rejoice to see them swept off the face of the earth—driven out from their homes, wanderers and pariahs, to migrate to some distant region, or to swell the over-stocked labor force of the great cities, with all manner of temptations, pulling them down to crime and ruin. What would be thought of the farmer who, when told that a lion was ravaging and destroying his flocks and herds, would rub his hands and cry out "Bully for the lion! Give it to the darned cusses!" Why, the neighbors of that man would see that he was safely removed to the insane asylum. And is not this just what the middlemen are doing, in their contemptible crusade against their customers; in their upholding of every ring and trust and combine that plunders them? Does not every dollar stolen from the farmers leave a dollar less for the farmers to trade with at the stores? And yet, many of these peaked-nosed villagers actually persecute the farmers for their efforts to protect themselves, so that they may have something to take to that very merchant's store. Is it any wonder that the farmers are driven to consider whether it would not be well to get clear of the whole gang who live upon, and, nevertheless, hate and despise them? These townspeople will yet wake up to realize that the farmers are necessary to them, but that they are in no wise necessary to the farmers. Of course, there are here and there good, sensible merchants and business men, who understand these things, who have hearts under their waistcoats; who are ready to work for the benefit of the whole community; and who do not regard their customers as the tiger regards the poor Hindoo he devours, but as friends and brethren, whose well-being is essential to their own. The poet says, however:

> "There are good men here and there; but the world,
> Like a black block of marble, jagged with white,
> Looks blacker than without such."

Now, my dear father, I want you never to forget the years of desperate misery you passed through:—the hopeless, endless struggle against debt and high rates of interest, when every well-dressed man approaching the farm was looked upon by you and the whole family with terror, for he was presumably a lawyer, a banker, or a sheriff's officer. Stop and think what it means in a community when all the well-dressed men live off the people, while the people themselves, the source of all wealth, are steeped to the lips in debt and poverty. Why, you know very well that, in some sections, a buggy is enough to throw a whole community of western farmers into a paroxysm of terror. A farmer in a good suit of clothes is so rare a sight in much of the western United States that the presumption is he was a member of the last legislature, and got a divide with the giant plunderers of the people. For as pork is fried in its own fat, so the people are controlled and kept in subjection by a tithe of the wealth stolen from them. This it is that runs the old parties; pays the expenses of the lawyers, bankers, machine agents, insurance agents, etc., who constitute the old party conventions; and buys up the members of the legislature, whose salaries are paid by the people, and whose principal business it is to betray the people, and deny them the very legislation they demand. And now, to think that you—my father—the other day the poorest of the poor—made rich by an extraordinary freak of fortune, and an intervention of Divine Providence—should at once join in to oppress the very class from which you have risen, and grind them still farther down into the earth; and should complain of the prosperity I have created around you, and be ready to remove to a distant town to find miserable victims for your greed.

Darwin says mankind are descended from monkeys. It is an insult to the monkeys to say so. And I should not wonder if that is what they are chattering about so vociferously and persistently in the menageries. If their language could be interpreted, it would probably be found that they are vigorously protesting that they are not the ancestors of those vicious, cruel, greedy beasts called men.

No, my dear father; I am ready to respond to any reasonable demands for your personal happiness and comfort, but I shall not give you one cent with which to make others wretched. Respectfully your son,

EPHRAIM BENEZET.

CHAPTER XVI.

ARCHIBALD M. HAYES' LETTER.

THE next letter I opened was from my excellent friend the attorney, Mr. Hayes. It read as follows:

MY DEAR SIR:—I beg leave to report to you the results of the trust you were good enough to leave in my hands.

I have been exceedingly busy: an immense crowd is constantly gathered in and around my office; the street is, at times, almost impassable. Many come to obtain loans, but the greater number desire simply to record their names, so that when their existing mortgages fall due, months or years ahead, they may be able to secure loans from you. I enclose you a tabulated statement of the amount already put out, with the name of each borrower, the sum lent, a description of the property, etc. You will perceive that the total amount loaned for you, to this date, is four hundred and seventy-six thousand eight hundred dollars. I hold all the notes and mortgages subject to your order—they are drawn to you. The total amount of existing mortgage indebtedness, at the time you began to make loans in this county, as shown by the register of deed books, was one million six hundred and twenty-eight thousand dollars, all of it bearing ten per cent per annum interest, with bonus on loan or for renewals of as much more, making a total of three hundred and twenty-five thousand dollars per annum taken out of industry in this one county every year, besides the stealages on the watered stock of railroad companies, which, as I figure it, amounts to about as much more; and besides the chattel-mortgage indebtedness, the store bills, machine bills, etc., etc., all of it bearing interest from ten to forty per cent. Every year these vast sums had to be wrung from about two thousand farmers; they had to toil unceasingly to raise it; and when they had paid it there was left to them only the means of the barest and rudest subsistence. Now, thanks to your great and unparalleled charity, the three hundred and twenty-five thousand dollars will be reduced to thirty-two thousand five hundred dollars per annum, and this will leave nearly three hundred thousand dollars annually in the hands of the producing class. With this they will soon pay up their chattel-mortgage indebtedness, their store debts, their machine debts, etc., and then the annual saving will be applied to increasing the comforts of their homes, and to paying off gradually the principal of their mortgages.

I cannot begin to describe to you the transformation already wought in the appearance of the people of this county.

Their whole aspect has changed. Hope has lighted up their hearts; their eyes are bright; their faces smiling. Men and women have gone to work with redoubled energy; and you know our American people are the most energetic and industrious in the world; and those emigrants who have come to us from foreign lands are but little behind them. They feel assured that their homes are saved. The dreadful doubt as to the future, which ate like a coal of fire into their hearts all these years, is gone. They can not only see the clouds rising from the earth; they already behold the sun of hope shining in the heavens. The gloom and dejection are all gone. They move with quicker steps. They are better fed, and that means greater capacity to work.

The strangest part of the affair is the effect of this change upon the business men of the town, and the town itself. At first the villagers would have hung you. They prophesied the utter destruction of everything. But as soon as the farmers, who borrowed from you, realized that they had a surplus to spend, which before went to the money-lender, they found they had a thousand wants. There was a new fence or a new barn to be built; the men's and women's clothes were worn threadbare, and had to be replaced; articles of furniture were to be bought; they must have a new harness for the team, and something of the luxuries of civilization for the table. Those who had not yet borrowed from you, but had entered their names for loans, felt so sure of an increased income in a few months or a year or two, that they had more courage to go in debt, and the merchants felt safer in giving them credit. The business of the town quadrupled in a month. The streets were lined with wagons; every store was packed with buyers; the wholesale merchants in Kansas City were so astounded by the magnitude of the orders from our town, for goods, that they were afraid at first to ship the goods, until they sent an agent out to investigate the cause of such an extraordinary demand; but when they learned the facts, every merchant here could get all the credit he wanted on his own terms. The merchants and business men made money "hand over fist;" and they set carpenters and painters and masons at work repairing their houses or erecting new and grander ones. There were no more mortgage foreclosures in the weekly paper, but the merchants advertised so liberally that the happy editor had to enlarge his journal; and, released from the thraldom of his indebtedness of a few dollars to a banker, the better elements of the man came to the top, and he has become a defender of popular rights and the demands of the Alliance. The news spread, and business men and mechanics from other localities rushed for this centre of activity and happiness; and we have greatly increased our population: town lots have had a "boom," and even the lawyers are kept busy drawing deeds and contracts; and they at last realize that there can be prosperity, even for them, that is not based on the impoverishment and ruin of their fellow-men.

The whole town is happy; and the men who intended to have sent you to the insane asylum are now collecting money to erect a monument to you as a great public benefactor; and they propose to place it in the most prominent part of the town. Even the bankers, who shook the dust of the place from their feet, and left us forever, have heard the news and returned to share in the general prosperity; and one of them told me the other day that really there was more money to be made where all were making money than where the most of the people were going to destruction. They are like Charles Lamb's Chinamen, who, after burning up hundreds of houses over the owners' heads, in order to roast the owner's pigs, discovered, to their intense astonishment and delight, that they could actually roast a pig without burning a house. And so these men have at last learned that they can positively make money without sending some poor fellow-being to a pauper's grave; in other words, that business does not mean a kind of moral murder.

I know it must be a great pleasure for you to hear all this, and to realize that you have conferred so much happiness upon so many thousands of worthy human creatures. It has been, I assure you, a great pleasure to me to be the humble instrument of doing all this good under your directions. I hope you will command my services in all things in the future.

Our townspeople have only one dread upon their minds, and it really begins to look as if it was well founded. This county is an oasis of happiness in the midst of a wide desert of human misery, more than two thousand miles in diameter. As the fame of our prosperity spreads, the unhappy people all round us will move in upon us; and then their ever-increasing competition will crush out our business men and our mechanics and laboring men, until we, the townspeople, will be once more reduced to the level of the general misery. Can you not, my dear sir, use the influence your great wealth and benevolence have given you, to induce Congress, now in session, to do for the whole nation what you have done for a single county, and thus lift the entire Republic out of the slough of wretchedness in which it is now wallowing? Pardon the suggestion; but I perceive that it is useless to help one spot if all the rest of the land is left unredeemed. It is like shipwrecked sailors who, in their despair, swim to the plank that already holds up one man, and is not large enough to sustain any others; and clambering upon it, they all go down to the bottom together. But Congress could give this universal relief, and only Congress can do it. Believe me to be, with great respect, your humble friend

ARCHIBALD M. HAYES.

CHAPTER XVII.

I APPEAL TO CONGRESS.

Mr. Hayes' suggestion set me to thinking seriously.

I was the most talked-of man in the nation. The newspapers chronicled my slightest movement. Ten thousand scientists were engaged in all parts of the world searching for "the philosopher's stone." The business classes were literally down on their knees before me; the bankers worshipped me; the newspapers glorified me as never king or emperor had been glorified before in all this world.

I could make gold! I could make millions in an instant!

Was there ever such a power? What were the periods of the grandest orator, the strains of the noblest poet, compared with the power to make gold? What were beauty, art, literature, music, painting, statecraft, in comparison with the unlimited ownership of the universal yellow master of mankind! The goldmaker! I could have established a religion, and all men would have worshipped me!

What could I not accomplish? For the people had confidence in me. They had read of my marriage to Sophie; and of Sophie's great society for the redemption of women; and of the transformation of Butler County, Kansas; and we were the most popular couple in the world. All the newspaper type in creation was busy praising us both.

Did it not seem reasonable, therefore, that if, with all this prestige, I went down to Washington, and made a speech to Congress, they would do what I proposed? Why not? I would try it.

And so I telephoned that I wanted to see the reporters of the daily press.

In an hour fifty forward-leaning, eager-faced young men, with pencil and paper in hand, bright, keen, honorable, sagacious youths, sat around me in my parlor, ready to convey to an expectant world my every word, my lightest whisper, the movement of my lips, the wrinkle of my brows, with a photographic description of my whole person, from the top of my head to the soles of my boots, illustrated with bright, vivacious pencil sketches of my appearance, my house, everything.

I told them what I wanted. The pencils flew. I desired to talk to Congress upon the money question; to urge upon them land loans to the people, at *two per cent per annum.*

The next day the whole civilized world was talking about and generally approving of my grand ideas; for could anything less than grand ideas emanate from *a man who could make gold!* If I had cried "*Boo!*" on the street corners, mankind would have seen some occult, mysterious, and prophetic meaning in that wondrous syllable. They would have recognized it as an embodiment of the incalculable; a symbol of the infinite and the inexpressible.

My journey to Washington was like the movement of the giant Gulliver through the land of the Liliputians. It was one continued ovation. An angel from heaven, who could not create gold, would have been, with all his wings, a very tame and uninteresting personage compared with me. A few philosophers might have examined him to see how his quill feathers were attached to him, but his heavenly whiteness would have been left standing alone, while rich and poor, princes and peasants, bankers and beggars, "rag-tag and bob-tail," and all mankind, would have poured swarming and howling after the gold-maker.

Surely, I thought, Congress will go down on its knees before me, and I shall save the country.

At Washington it took a corps of twenty policemen to fight a way for me through the dense mob, many acres in extent, which assembled at the depot. I lost my hat in the *mêlée*, and it was instantly torn into a thousand shreds, and distributed among the multitude as sacred relics. The possessors, like the men who had a single hair from Julius Cæsar's head,

> "Would dying mention it within their will;
> Bequeathing it, as a rich legacy,
> Unto their issue."

For what was Julius Cæsar, and all his conquests, compared with a man who could make gold!

I dined with the President at the White House—a state dinner in my honor; one of those intellectual exhibitions interrupted by food; a commingling of the "feed" of our gluttonous ancestors with the literary lyceum and debating society of our modern civilization; neither perfect eating nor perfect thinking, but an incongruous mixture of both; belly and brains stirred together in a kind of uncomfortable suet pudding.

I spoke in the great chamber of the House of Representatives. Everything that was talented or brilliant or handsome or learned in the Capitol City was present. Every inch of space was crammed with people. The cheering lasted for five minutes as I rose. I make some extracts from the short-hand report which appeared, the next day, in the Associated Press dispatches:

FELLOW-CITIZENS: I come to speak to you, as the law-making power, about the welfare of the people.

No higher theme could occupy you or me.

The Constitution of the United States declares the "welfare" of the people to be one of the supreme purposes for which that instrument and our government were formed. It is, indeed, the only purpose that can justify the existence of government and the collection of taxes. It is absurd to think that any intelligent people would submit to the limitations, restraints, and exactions of government if they did not expect to receive in return an improvement of their material condition. Any other theory implies that the mass of mankind are fools; and if fools, they are incapable of self-government; and if this be so, you have no business here as the representatives of a conglomerate array of incapable people. [Laughter and applause.]

In the old times men carved, out of wood and stone, figures of men, and called them gods, and prostrated themselves before them, and worshipped the work of their own hands. In modern times men create governments for the good of mankind, and then sacrifice mankind for the good of the governments. They cannot see the people behind the tissue of articles and sections and provisos of the Constitution; and yet for the people was the whole thing created. This, as the great poet and thinker says, "is to make the worship greater than the god." This is to make the clothes greater than the man; the casket more valuable than the gem; the body more important than the soul; the universe mightier than its Creator. [Applause.]

Statutes, ordinances, customs; banks, bonds, money; beliefs, theories, religions; philosophies, dogmas, and doctrines, are only valuable as they conserve the happiness of mankind. Whenever they conflict with it, they must fall to the ground. Man is the only thing worth considering in this great world. He is the climax of the creative force; the ultimate object for which this planet was made; a little god working out the purposes of the great God. To set up anything—any device or invention of man, any belief or form or theory, statute or custom, against the welfare, happiness, development, of man—is a species of horrible blasphemy against the Everlasting One, whose child and instrument man is. Every cruelty to man thrills and shocks the universe, and all the angels in Heaven weep over his miseries. The injustice of the human creature to his fellow is the one unforgivable sin, for which a hundred hells of remorse exist throughout the incalculable ages. [Cheers.]

Is man happy under this American government? No.

I need not enter into statistics. Every newspaper abounds with them. You all know that cunning has thriven while toil has starved. To those that had, has been given; while from those who had not, has been taken away even that little which they had. A flood of debt, as huge as that of water in which Noah floated, covers the whole land. If the downpour is not stopped, it will soon stand fathoms deep over the highest mountain-peaks of human endeavor. Already millions of our noblest workers have been swept from the face of the land and their possessions given to strangers. A mighty transformation has taken place in the last quarter of a century. The country is becoming unfit to sustain a republic, and busy mites are at work laying the foundations of despotism. The yeomanry are disappearing, as they long ago disappeared from the face of Europe. Goldwin Smith said during our Civil War: "Where are now the yeomanry of England? Where are now the small holders of land who at Naseby and Marston Moor, under the lead of Cromwell, struck conquering blows for liberty, and brought the head of a king to the block? Gone—gone from England forever. Seek out their posterity. Where are they? On the plains of America, in the valley of the Mississippi, marching under the banners of Grant and Sherman." [Applause.]

Where are those soldiers now? A large part of them are already obliterated from the face of the land they defended; together with the other gallant men who fought under Lee and Stonewall Jackson; while the rest stand knee-deep or waist-deep, watching the steady rise of the black and dreadful waters of misfortune that will soon rise to their lips, and sweep them into the abyss. [Cheers.]

And when swept off their homes, where are these yeomen to go? Where are their children to go? Are there any more Americas for a new Columbus to discover? No; this is the last camping-ground of the human family. Beyond the Pacific are the densely peopled lands of the Orient—China, Japan, India—already supporting all the population they can maintain. The waves of migration, which started ten thouands years ago from Atlantis, have reached their last limits of expansion, east and west. To yield up the land now is to yield up everything; to fail now is to fail for eternity. We stand at the parting of the ways. From this eminence we can behold the future. Shall our posterity be freemen or slaves? Shall they be civilized, cultured denizens of a happy earth, where all forces are conjoined for the good of man; or shall they be barbarian toilers, ruled by civilized masters in a hell of unrequited labor and injustice? [Great applause.]

We boil down the history of the planet into this one question: Shall the soil of the earth be subdivided among the many, or shall it be concentrated in the hands of the few? [Cheers.]

Once lost to the many, it can never be regained from the few. Once lost, there goes with it dignity, prosperity, happiness, independence, civilization, republican institutions.

Is the land passing from the many to the few? You know it is. The central West was settled mainly by bankrupt farmers from the States farther east; the squeezed-out, mortgage-ruined farmers of the central West have poured in one great flood into Nebraska, the Dakotas, Wyoming, etc. And these again, under the same pressure, are flooding Utah, Montana, Idaho, and the Pacific Coast. Already the vanguard catches sight of the blue waters of the planet's greatest ocean; already, like buffaloes urged forward to the yawning precipice, they look back over their shoulders at the oncoming rush of the dispossessed millions, swarming behind them. And as the great army of the disappointed and the unhappy thus marches forward across a continent, the scattered picket line of Capital advances silently, and takes possession of the abandoned homesteads, and the great Republic is transformed, lost, ruined. Where sturdy yeomanry once raised stalwart boys and girls, with the mettle of soldiers and heroines, a cringing tenantry eats its bread in shame and submission. And down drops in rotting silence the mighty Republic, like a giant that, in the very prime of manhood, perishes of white and scaly leprosy, shaking the dust of pestilence athwart the world, with every movement of his enfeebled limbs. [Cheers.]

Will you stand still, O men and brothers, and see the noble nation perish—the God-adorned, the illustrious, the transendent nation—the foremost glory of this world—the poor man's nation, the yeoman's republic, founded by fishers and ploughers and hunters, by men in homespun and deerskin? [Cries of "No, no," and great cheering.] Will not those old bones—those brawny, giant bones of heroes—rise from their graves, from Bunker Hill to Cowpens, with the shreds of the "ragged regimentals" clinging to them, and form in line, their rusty weapons in hand, to defend the life of the Republic, threatened by the indifference of a corrupt, degraded, and pigmy age? [Great applause.]

And how can you save it?

Keep the land in the hands of the many. [Cheers.]

Limit the amount that any man may own. [Cheers.]

See to it that the working-men obtain homes. [Great cheers.]

Use the powers of government for the good of the governed. [Cheers.]

Open the post-offices as savings banks, as other countries have done. There is little difference between depositing fifty dollars, as we do now, in a post-office, and receiving an order payable at any other post-office, and depositing that same fifty dollars and receiving a government agreement to repay that sum any time after thirty days, at any post-office in the United States, with two per cent per annum interest added. [Great applause.]

There are now one billion and a half dollars in the savings banks of this country. Do this, and every dollar of it would in a short time be deposited in the post-offices, with billions more which the people do not dare to trust to the banks, but have hidden away or buried in the earth.

But what will the government do with all this vast sum, many times larger than our whole national debt? The answer is plain. Lend it out to the farmers and working-men on real-estate security, at two per cent per annum, to enable them to save or obtain homes; to break the backs of the usurers, and prevent the transformation of this country from a republic into a despotism. [Tremendous applause.]

Nay, go farther. Issue paper currency, legal-tender, to the amount of fifty dollars *per capita.* [Immense applause.] Man is now a "drug," and money is a god. Let us reverse it. Let us make money a "drug" and man a god. [Great cheering.] Money was invented for man's use. Man was not created for money's use. [Applause.] One farmer who raises a hundred bushels of wheat, or a bale of cotton; or one mechanic who turns ten dollars' worth of steel into a thousand dollars of manufactures, has done more for mankind than all Wall Street. [Great applause.] He has added something to the real wealth of the world—something to eat, something to wear, something to use—while Wall Street has produced nothing but ruin. Lock up a hundred bankers in a cellar without food; give them all the gold of Threadneedle Street; and come back in a week, and they will look like the remains of a Greely expedition to the North Pole—a ghastly array of picked bones and starving maniacs. [Great laughter and applause.] Ask the survivors what real wealth is, and they will tell you that they would exchange Golconda for a loaf of bread. Oh, the sin and shame of it, that the real producers of real wealth are crushed and degraded by the possessors of a couple of metals, with scarcely any intrinsic value, but rendered sacred by a prehistoric superstition. They have stolen the "measures of value," and converted them into beasts, that breed faster than any creature that God ever made. [Great applause.]

The whole thing is wrong. Barbarian man had no money; he knew nothing but "*barter.*" He swapped an arrow-head for an orange; a sea-shell ornament for a piece of venison. It was religion that rendered gold and silver valuable by making them sacred, dedicating them to the worship of the sun and moon. The yellow metal was consecrated to the yellow god of day; the white metal to the pale mistress of the night. They were in demand on all barbaric and civilized coasts, and therefore exchangeable for all things valuable to man. Hence they became money. But it was still and is yet merely a kind of *barter.* It is easier to handle one hundred dollars' worth of these compact metals than the same value of wheat or meat or cattle. And so to this hour the world's commerce is based on a swapping of commodities; the religious, metallic, prehistoric emblems for those things that man has to eat or wear or use, and which are therefore real wealth. Let two men be shipwrecked on a desert island, one with a bag of gold and the other with a bag of flour. In forty-eight hours the possessor of the gold would realize its purely artificial, conventional character; its utter uselessness to man in a state of nature; and would be willing to swap his whole wealth for a "square meal" out of the other man's sack. [Great laughter and applause.]

Supreme hunger would dissolve the prehistoric, religious traditions of the sun and moon worship, into the thinnest of thin air. [Cheers.]

Let us get clear of all this nonsense. Let us relegate the worship of gold and silver to the region of witchcraft and spooks, and all the other trash of the under-fed, undeveloped past. Let us establish several propositions:

1. That real money is not a commodity, but a governmental measure of values, to facilitate the exchange of commodities.

2. That the government must furnish its people with an adequate supply of this medium of exchange, just as it is in duty bound to furnish them with an adequate supply of postage stamps.

3. That this medium should bear the government stamp and be full legal-tender for all debts public and private; otherwise it is not money, but disqualified rubbish.

4. That it should be made of the cheapest and lightest material, with a reasonable degree of durability; and these qualities we find in paper.

5. That it should be so abundant as to enable the community to do business on a cash basis, and not pay interest on the bulk of its transactions.

Think of postage stamps being so scarce that we could not obtain them except by buying them from the bank at an increased price. And the fewer there were of them the higher the price would go; communication between the people would be interrupted, and finally a man would have to mortgage a cow to get a dollar's worth of postage stamps. Then imagine the banks corrupting Congress to maintain their monopoly, and you will have a pretty fair conception of our present financial slavery. [Applause.]

Look at the effects of a cheap and abundant currency in the county of Butler, Kansas. [Tremendous cheering.] See how prosperity and the beauty of human life and the glory of industry have been restored to that people. [Applause.] See how vice has been reduced to a minimum. [Applause.] But that county is only an island of happiness in the midst of an ocean of misery, which will soon rise and overwhelm it. Poverty is a pestilence which has no respect for national, state, or county lines. It moves upon the air until it reduces all things to its own level. To relieve the county we must lift up the state; to give prosperity to the state we must see to it that justice is done in the nation; to permanently help the nation *we must strike down the robbery of mankind in all the lands of the earth.* [Tremendous cheering, long continued.]

The nation must do for all Kansas and for all the states and for all the world what I have done for Butler County, Kansas. [Applause.]

And what a splendid prospect unrolls before before my eyes! A whole nation prosperous; happy, laughing faces looking out from the Atlantic coast as the sun rises over the fisher's boats; laughing faces looking out over the Pacific as the golden rays of sunset flash from the bosom of the dancing waters. [Cheers.] In all the plains and valleys, on all the hills and mountains, prosperity, happiness; money a drug and man glorified and glorious; while art, religion, literature, science, rise triumphant, splendid, from the ashes of a land but yesterday enslaved and ruined. [Great cheering.]

And you—ye law-makers—why do ye not do this thing? What is it restrains you? You are the people, and the people are supreme. Why should they hesitate to give themselves universal prosperity? What old-world theory, what interest of a class, can stand in the way of the happiness of the people and the preservation of the Republic? The people pay you your salaries; they hire you to make laws for *their* benefit, not for the benefit of any class that preys upon them. You are sworn to support the Constitution of the United States, and that Constitution declares that its object is "*to promote the general welfare.*" [Tremendous cheering.] Go forward! Use the unparalleled power which God and the nation's battle-fields have placed in your hands for the good of mankind.

At the end of this speech the audience went wild. I had a perfect ovation. I returned to my hotel accompanied by a swarming multitude of friends and admirers, and happy in the belief that I had converted Congress, and that laws would be at once passed to accomplish the reforms I had demanded.

Ah! little did I realize that Plutocracy was not yet conquered; that it held all popular convictions, uproars, excitements, in contempt; and that it possessed weapons in its great armory of which the common people knew nothing.

CHAPTER XVIII.

HOW PLUTOCRACY WORKED.

WHILE I smiled and exulted the conspirators were at work.

The first symptom was that the great newspapers reported my speech without any comments.

But in a day or two the New York journals gave the clew for the country press. Democratic and Republican sheets sang the same song and told the same story in every part of the Union. It was a Hydra with ten thousand mouths and only one voice.

"It would take three billion dollars of currency to carry out my ideas; the faith and credit of the nation would not uphold so vast a sum," they cried in unison.

I replied by asking the question, whether the faith and credit of the nation were not equal to the task of upholding three billion dollars of national bonds at par? Would not the world buy them up at once, if offered for sale? Did not the industry of the people uphold the value of five billion dollars of watered stock of railroad companies, which did not represent one dollar of actual capital ever invested, or that ever would be invested; and yet the toil of the people paid the interest on all that vast sum, without the slightest hope of any equivalent? Did not the watered stock on railroads, telegraphs, mills, etc., amount to *thirteen billions!* Did not the industry of our people, besides these terrible and unjust burdens, pay the interest on many other billions of individual indebtedness?

But the newspapers replied:

"The government notes would fall in price to fifty cents on the dollar. There can scarcely be a surplus of bonds; the capacity of the population to pay interest is the sole limit of credit in that direction; but if you put out more money than the business of the country demands it must fall in value."

To this I replied:

"Then let us create a system of interchangeable bonds and currency. Whenever the paper money falls below its face value, give the holder of a thousand dollars the right to exchange it for a thousand dollar bond, bearing one per cent interest, payable at the option of the government, at any time, in legal tender notes. If, then, the credit of the nation is sufficient to uphold a bond while it will not uphold a bank note, the bond will sustain the note, if they are interchangeable. And what the government will lose in interest on the bonds, for a year or two, will be more than made up by the resulting prosperity of the whole people, and their increased capacity to pay more taxes to meet that interest.

"If the bonds and notes are of the same value, there

will be no inducement to exchange the notes for bonds. If there are some who have no immediate use for their $1,000, and desire to put it into a bond so as to get the $10 on it at the end of the year, there will be others who will need money in their business, and they will turn their bonds into currency. And the government can prevent a great accumulation of bonded debt by taking up the bonds by new issues of currency. It is nonsense to suppose that a great and ingenious people cannot invent some system that will keep their paper money at par.

"Nor will it do to say that the business of the country will not absorb fifty dollars *per capita*. We are increasing in population at the rate of nearly one-third every ten years; the coat that is too big for a boy will be just large enough for that boy grown into a man; the amount of currency that may not be demanded by the business necessities of sixty-five million people, will be all required in ten years by eighty-four million people. Moreover, the amount of currency demanded is not to be estimated upon the basis of population, but of enterprise, activity, wealth. A Russian village of peasants, living at a cost of seventy cents per month, will not need one-thousandth part of the currency demanded by the people of a rushing, growing, pushing, western American city.

"Neither must it be forgotten that all new issues of statecraft must be treated tentatively. We have never before had, in the history of the world, just such conditions as surround us now. Never has such a vast population, so highly civilized, been rapidly expanded under one government, with all the appliances of the highest social development, over a continent. Old-world forms, beliefs, and theories cannot apply to us. Our gold and silver money has been inherited by us as we inherited the belief in witchcraft and sorcery. As a form of *barter* those metals were well enough for small subdivisions of misgoverned country, where the condition of the people was wretched enough at the best. But here we are with a *world* to provide for. The child is born that will live to see this nation possessed of two hundred and fifty millions of population, with an incredible amount of wealth; vaster, probably, than that of all Europe and all the Orient to-day. It is absurd to suppose that the business of such a tremendous nation can be permanently tied to the apron-strings of two metals, gold and silver; whose supply is diminishing relatively to population, and may utterly cease in a few years, and we go to destruction, just as Roman civilization broke down from the exhaustion of the mines of Spain. God never intended that mankind, with all its vast capacity for expansion and evolution upward, should continue forever the bond-slave of two out of many hundred metals, simply because some dead-and-gone priesthood, in the remote backward abysm and gulf of prehistoric time, by some accident associated those metals with their belief that the sun and moon were living gods, and the creators of all things terrestrial and celestial. It would be the sheerest and shallowest bigotry and a disgrace to the intelligence of civilized man, who has outgrown so many other of the senseless superstitions of his ancestors.

"We must dissociate from the governmental measure of values, from the yard-stick of prices, employed to facilitate the exchange of those commodities which are useful to man (and those and those alone constitute real wealth), the accidental, traditional, and conventional value given to these two metals, gold and silver, which in themselves have very little real value. We must divorce the new civilization from the old superstition. We must separate *fiat* from commodity. We must use the power of the aggregated community, which we call government, and which is the greatest power on earth, to furnish a medium of exchange, to enable the people to *swap* what they produce with one another; without a man, for instance, who trades off a bullock for dry goods, groceries, books and hardware, being compelled to cut up the animal into bits, and give each dealer a subdivision of it.

"But in issuing governmental money in large quantities, we should proceed, as I say, tentatively. We should feel our way, as an elephant crosses a bridge; advancing only so fast as we can advance with safety; taking into consideration not only the existing conditions which surround us, but that very potent factor, only to be obliterated by experience, the prejudices of mankind. We can decide in advance what direction we will travel in, but we must leave it to the condition of the road to determine how fast we shall advance. We will finally reach the goal if we continue to go forward, if we do not precipitate ourselves into the swamps of rashness and inexperience. But we *must* furnish this mighty population, and the still mightier populations that are to come after us, a medium of exchange that can be expanded *pari passu* with the growth of population, wealth, and business of the whole country. Gold and silver will not answer our purpose. *Civilization has only been maintained by the invention of paper money.* Experience may show that we have already opened the last gold and silver mines on the planet. The Mohammedans have a fast which extends from sunrise to sunset. But if they were transplanted to the Arctic circle, where the day is six months long, they would either have to give up their superstition or their lives. The Koran did not contemplate the possibility of such geographical conditions. The petty nations of Europe, of the past, half hinds and half brutes, with a commerce scarcely distinguishable from piracy, when they made the *sacred* metals of a still more remote antiquity their *precious* metals, and used them for money, did not forsee this vast America, where more business is transacted in a year than they knew of in many centuries; and which is occupied by a people so intelligent that the poorest workman knows more than did their emperors and clergymen. We must expand our thoughts to the measure of our greatness. We must turn our faces to the future, not to the past."

Of course these utterances of mine were greedily snatched up by the reporters and published in all the papers.

The chorus of newspapers replied by talking of the French assignats, the American continental shinplasters, etc.

I replied that the conditions of the American people to-day were vastly different from those of the nations referred to. "Who would compare the French people, unaccustomed to self-government, rising blood-boltered from its terrible battle with feudalism, to this august, peaceful, long-established nation, with whom republican institutions are an instinct, and an established and undoubted fact? Who would institute a parallel between the three or four millions of poor colonists, stretched along tide-water on our Atlantic coast, repudiating the price of their victory because of their very necessities and miseries, and this majestic nation, soon to hold one hundred million inhabitants?"

But the chorus replied that abundant currency was simply a stepping-stone to land loans, for in no other way could the money be gotten out among the people, for existing revenues were adequate for all the expenses of the nation.

"And why not?" I answered. "What were the national bank notes, but a loan of government paper on the security of government bonds? When the system was established it was upon the ground that the credit of the national government, engaged in a terrible civil war of which no man could foresee the outcome, was not strong enough to float government money, but the credit of the nation must be supplemented by the credit of rich men in every town and city. This was the theory. But that condition has long since passed away. This nation to-day needs no indorser. Now the national banker is practically a borrower from the government. He deposits one hundred thousand dollars of bonds with the treasurer of the United States, and the treasurer *lends* him ninety thousand dollars of notes, free of all charge, (except his share of the taxes which all must pay); the government prints the notes and hands them out to him, and the banker takes them home and lends them out; and most of them are soon loaned out on land, at high rates of interest; or loaned to merchants who depend upon the farms of the people for that production of real wealth that will enable them to carry on business. For every one knows that everything in this world comes from the land: food, clothes, tools, ores, fuel, houses, everything. There isn't anything real and abiding but the planet itself, and therefore its surface is called *real* estate.

"If the land is sufficient security for the loan of those government notes in the hands of the banker, why should it not be sufficient security for those notes without passing through the hands of the banker? We have three elements: government, banker, land.

Which are the most important? Wipe out the middle element, is not everything substantial left: government and land? Is there anything in the world more tangible and actual than government and land? The one can take your life, and the other you cannot live without. Wherein is the banker essential to government or the planet?

"But the banker protests vigorously against being eliminated in that way; against being suspended in mid-air, like Mahomet's coffin, unattached to either government or the planet. And his kickings and strugglings, to hold on to the government with one hand and the planet with the other, constitutes a large part of what we call old-party politics. It is for these objects that conventions assemble, elections are held, and congresses are corrupted."

"But," cried the newspapers, "you would debase the currency of the country!"

"Not necessarily," I replied, "we would, by careful experimentation, determine what volume of the currency of a country could be kept at par by the taxes that are payable in that currency. In other words, as the banker by keeping in his vaults one dollar of specie is able to maintain three dollars of his paper at par, can a nation issue three times as much currency as the amount to be paid annually in taxes, state, county, city and national? If this be so, can it issue six times as much; can it issue ten times as much? These are questions that are only to be settled in the arena of actual experience.

"But if there is any risk of a debased currency, which, I would ask, is the greatest national calamity—a debased currency or a debased people? We were the most prosperous nation in the world, immediately after the Civil War, with gold at a large premium. As our currency rose, our people went down. But we cannot maintain republican institutions among a debased people. When the land is all concentrated in the hands of the few, a standing army will be needed to keep the discontented serfs in subjection; and a king will be needed to command the standing army; and a nobility to sustain the king; and America becomes Europe. Joshua, we are told, made the sun stand still; our new Joshua, the money power, will send the sun rushing backward, while all the solar system goes howling to destruction. The last census shows that nearly one-fourth the farmers of the United States are already tenants; the whole number of cultivators of the soil is 4,225,955, and of these 1,024,701 are renters. In 1850 the farmers of the United States owned five-eighths of the total wealth of the nation; in 1860 they owned less than one-half; in 1870 a little over one-third; in 1880 a little over one-fourth; *in 1890 less than one-fifth!* WHAT WILL BE THEIR SHARE IN 1900? Answer that terrible question.

"Which is more important—Wall Street or the nation; the money of the country or the people of the country; a financial theory or mankind?

"Which should we build up—the few or the many?

"Are not the *people* of more importance than continent or constitution? God made the planet for the people, not the people for the money-lenders. To stand still and see the people reduced to serfdom would be a crime against God and man. Better that all the gold and silver in the world should perish than that the nation should die; better that we should go back to primeval barter, without a dollar of money of any kind, than see God's children wiped off the face of God's planet. Ancient Mexico maintained a high civilization without a particle of money. If driven to the dreadful alternative of losing liberty and prosperity or metallic money, no sane man can doubt which the nation should choose. It is the curse of the world that mankind has been ruled for centuries by money, in the interest of money; not by the people in the interest of the people. We live only half-way in the present. The age is like a reptile whose head projects, lifted and gasping, out of the carbonic acid gas; but its nether limbs are yet imbedded in the thick mud of the Silurian period. Man has all antiquity sitting on his coat-tails, and his hardest task is to go forward; he wades, waist-deep, in the obstruction of his own prejudices and bigotries. The noble, God-given light of intelligence is shut up in a boy's carved calabash-lantern, and casts only grotesque and hideous figures on the mud; while the hard grass-grown paths of original thought stretch before him unheeded. Man rarely asks, What is it possible for me to do? But his inquiry always is—What have my predecessors done?"

"But," said another, "why all this clamor for an abundant currency? What difference does it make? Suppose money was so scarce that fifty cents paid a man's wages, instead of one dollar. What difference would that make to the workman, if everything else in the world was reduced one-half in price?"

"That is plausible," I replied, "but let us apply the *reductio ad absurdum* to it; if it does no harm to reduce the workman's wages, and all things else, from one dollar to fifty cents, what harm would it do to reduce it to ten cents, or one cent; or to utterly wipe out all money? But while the money is rising in purchasing power through its increasing scarcity, all forms of property are falling. The world is on a 'down-grade'—it is eventually a bankrupt age. Every shrinkage of volume of money concentrates more and more of the possessions of the race in the hands of a few; and we gravitate toward the condition of Europe in the Middle Ages, when a penny paid a man's wages, and a sheep was worth twopence. The human mind stood still for hundreds of years, and mankind was divided into but two classes—brutal lords and still more brutal serfs. No, no; the world does not want to travel backward."

I thought I had the best of the argument, and the people thought so too. But the Plutocracy did not depend on newspaper articles. Those were simply the ornamental icing of the cake; the substantial part of the pastry was below.

The House passed my bill with a great hurrah of popular enthusiasm. And the country rejoiced.

The bill went to the Senate.

A double-barrelled legislature is a cunning contrivance. The object being to prevent government by the people, two chambers give two chances; that which cannot be killed in one branch may be slaughtered in the other. It is like a man who, having survived the ministrations of one doctor and recovered, is at once placed in the hands of another and dies. Why should there be two doctors?

And, then there being a possibility that the people may enforce their demands through both House and Senate, there sits, above both, a king called a President, with power to annul the action of both; one man who knows more than sixty millions of people, of whom he was the other day an obscure member.

In other words, the people is a horrible monster which must be chained by both legs and neck.

But, lest the people should coerce House, Senate, and President to do something against the moneyed aristocracy, there is still another tribunal. A lot of lawyers, mainly selected by the great corporations, sit upon a bench, with old women's gowns upon them, with power to nullify House, Senate, President, and people. Oh, it is a beautiful contrivance to arrest progress and shackle liberty!

Tom Jefferson foretold that the Supreme Court of

the United States would eventually absorb into their hands all the power of the nation. They are rapidly doing it, and doing it in the interest of the moneyed aristocracy.

After the poor devil the people—the outlaw, the Pariah—has struggled through, with a chain on his right leg and a chain on his left leg, and another chain around his neck, and reaches the foot of the judicial throne, and lifts his hands for help and mercy, the court quietly slices his head off with a technicality; a smooth, swift, shining technicality; derived, perchance, from some villanous, ignorant barbarian who lived in England several hundred years ago.

Great is the Republic! Mighty is the self-governing nation, where law lives and the people perish! The roaring, struggling lion, helpless in the net of the hunter, with not even a mouse to nibble him free. Self-government, like a homœopathic medicine, run through many dilutions; the ten-thousandth trituration of public opinion, after the press, the corruptionists, the fools, the knaves, the House, the Senate, the President, and the Supreme Court have all got through with it.

God help the Republic! Nothing but God can get it out of its present scrape.

A Republic based on the conception that the people rule; are fit to rule; and ought to rule; with a government which prevents the people from ruling. A *non sequitur;* liberty with despotism in its belly; the spirit of 1776 with a worse demon than old George

III. inside of it; the Declaration of Independence wrapped up in "watered stock;" George Washington dead, and Jay Gould living! God help us!

But while I philosophized the Plutocrats were driving my calf through the cow-yard of the House into the corral of the Senate—the slaughter pen. And there they clapped chloroform—called a committee—to its nose, to stop any bawling; and it died peacefully and graciously; while every member of the Senate was in favor of it! !

Sixty-five million people on the one side and a small gang of knaves on the other—and the knaves won.

CHAPTER XIX.

I GET MAD.

Now I was mad. Mad all through. Mad all over.

I had not that amiable American frame of mind, the product of our high civilization, which patiently submits to gross injustice and looks around, with a smile, for a compensating chance to steal something. I still had the flavor of the Kansas mud on my boots, and in my soul. I was not fully civilized; there was a good deal of the aboriginal barbarian left in my composition. The men of 1776 had not emerged very far from the savage, hunter state; and so they gave us a nation and a republic. If they had possessed the cultured frame of our minds to-day, they would have regarded it as a species of insanity to think of going to war, barefooted and in rags, for eight years, for a principle. They would have taken the money the Revolution cost and loaned it out at high rates of interest, and wiped a lot of poor devils off the face of the earth, and called it national prosperity. You couldn't have dragged them away from John Bull and his aristocracy with a yoke of oxen. They are hungering and thirsting now to get back into his embrace. They would rather be kicked by a duke than kissed by a genius.

My first step was to send off this telegram:

ARCHIBALD M. HAYES, El Dorado, Kansas—Leave your business in the hands of a trusty agent and come here at once. EPHRAIM BENEZET.

Then I sent word to my excellent young friends, the reporters, who seem to have in their natures something of the lightning they employ to carry their messages; electrical men, with all the *snap* of youth and all the experience of men of the world; good fellows, too, and as honest as their masters will permit them to be; I sent word to them to come and see me.

What a galaxy gathered around me, each with his fingers, as it were, on the keyboard of a vast audience, themselves the phonographs and telephones of civilization! As Hamlet says of the players we can say of them: "Let them be well used; for they are the abstracts and brief chronicles of the time; after your death you were better have a bad epitaph, than the ill report while you lived."

"Gentlemen," I began, "I want you to tell the world that the 'Gold-maker' is about to do something unheard of, heretofore, in the history of mankind.

"The people are perishing for want of money; they have wealth, they can create that out of the soil, by their industry; but in the midst of their abundance, each one producing a hundred-fold more than he can consume, they are sinking into bankruptcy. The land is covered with a filthy scab, an eczema of mortgages, under which vermin swarm and fatten; the soil is concentrating in the hands of the few; the yeomen are becoming peasants, the land-owners tenants; the Republic is dying, the last hopes of mankind are flickering in the socket ere they go out in eternal night.

"God has intervened to save humanity. He has given me the means to lift up the world. Scourged on by the recreancy of the government and the arrogance of the ruling class, I have resolved to come to the relief of the wretched people.

"*Say to the nation that I am about to create gold enough to take up every mortgage in the United States.*

"I shall lend my money to the people on twenty years' time, at two per cent per annum!

"I shall establish great manufacturing cities where labor can congregate; and I shall advance enough to each workman to enable him to secure a house and garden. Instead of forcing labor to go to capital, I shall compel capital to come to labor.

"*I shall revolutionize the nation, yea, the world.*

"The moneyed class have bought up the Senate, blocked reform, and made a mockery of self-government. By the power of God I pass by them and over them to the lifting up of the whole people.

"Say to the people that I need an honest, faithful agent in every town and village to superintend my loans. I want men who have got some heart in them, not mere heartless intellects; for intellect in these latter days has grown like a monstrous wen and sucked the substance out of heart.

"Let them send their recommendations at once to me.

"The first to be served shall be those whose mortgages have already been foreclosed, but who still have a day of grace and a chance to redeem their homes.

"What I am after is the protection of *homes*, the protection of the roofs that shelter wives and little ones. These are the most precious things in all this world. I have no money for speculators, but for the mother and the babies everything."

CHAPTER XX.

THE GLAD TIDINGS OF GREAT JOY.

Lord! Lord! What rejoicing there was in all the land!

The people rang the church bells, bonfires were kindled, cannon boomed. From town to town the great wave of excitement and delight rolled like a flood, drowning out all sorrow. Who can count the millions of hearts that were rendered happy, the millions of wrinkles that were smoothed out of toil-worn faces, the millions of eyes, sunken and sad, that shone with the light of a great joy?

Mr. Hayes came. He was invaluable to me. We opened immense offices with thousands of clerks. The applications came in by the wagon-load.

Everything was reduced to a system.

At the suggestion of Mr. Hayes, I employed a force of detectives—guards. I brought into my laboratory piles of pig-iron. I replenished the chemicals. I closed the windows. I stationed my sentinels to keep away the curious and the criminal. I manufactured gold on a colossal scale. The teamsters were kept busy, under guard, hauling the bullion to the mint, and carrying the coin from the mint to the banks. I opened accounts with all the banks in Philadelphia, Boston, and New York.

Agents were employed in every village and city, and the golden flood began to pour fourth to all parts of the nation.

I cannot begin to describe the stupendous results. It was the experience of Butler County, Kansas, magnified a million-fold. The whole face of society was transformed. The vast aggregate of money which had been spent to pay interest on billions of dollars of debt, was gradually withdrawn from the pockets of an idle, non-producing class,—a few thousands in number—who had used the greater part of it to lend out again to others, thus swelling their wealth and the aggregate of human suffering—and it was left in the hands of the producers. But only for a little time did it stay there. Civilized man, educated, is as expansive as oxygen gas. His wants increase with his means. The greater part of the savings of the people went into the hands of the merchants, who made their percentage of profit off it; and then, after paying part to the farmers for food, they paid over the balance to the manufacturers; who, after deducting their profit, disbursed it among the working classes who made the goods; who, after taking out their share of happiness from it, and paying other farmers for food, paid it over once more to the merchants for the necessaries and luxuries of life; and these, in turn, paid it back to the manufacturers; who, in turn, gave another share to the laborers and the farmers; and so the dollars saved from the moneylenders penetrated to every part of the country, and to every fireside, moving with marvellous activity; and everywhere, like rain falling upon dry and dusty ground, this new supply of money, wherever it touched, caused enterprise, industry, joy, prosperity to spring up, like a noble crop of magnificent vegetation.

Millions of tons' weight of sorrow and fear and perplexity were lifted off the hearts of the toiling masses. In every direction the enterprise and zeal of the people extended itself. There were no more mortgage foreclosures; the courts stood idle; the criminal class decreased and almost disappeared; intemperance, the last grim refuge of the weak and miserable, became a thing of the past; even the mendicants rose to some sense of personal dignity as the pressure from above was withdrawn, and they found a chance to live without begging.

The whole moral nature of the people changed. They began to see that they had something to thank God for. It had been difficult indeed to worship God while the devil ruled the world. It had been difficult to cultivate sentiments of virtue while the gigantic rogues were the masters of society, and all men were prostrated before them. It had seemed in the past as if the wise man must necessarily be a villain, and only the fool was honest. Now all this was changed. The hands of God, overflowing with bounties, reached down to this nether world. The songs of praise welled up from all full hearts and overflowed from all smiling lips. Goodness was master once more of the universe.

And men laughed and wondered how it could have been possible that, for so many ages, mankind had permitted a few of their fellows to put snaffle-bits in their mouths and saddles on their backs, and ride them to destruction. They had been so long in a condition of debt, that it had seemed to them that the credit system was natural to mankind; born with them, as essential a part of their lives as their eyesight and hands. And they said to one another: "How stupid were we to permit, for all these centuries, this halt in the process of bartering our commodities, this break in the process of swapping our productions; in which, like robbers hiding in a cave by the roadside, the knaves have secreted themselves, ready to rush out and levy tribute upon every dollar of wealth that passed by them!" And they asked themselves: "Why were two commodities, gold and silver, permitted to establish a masterdom over all other commodities—yea, over all wealth and over all who produced wealth?" And the only answer was that it was that dreadful thing—the most dreadful that can take possession of the human mind—a superstitious adoration of the past; that belief in the beliefs of an ignorant and dead and buried ancestry, which has covered the world with wars and murders, has dwarfed the minds and darkened the souls of uncountable billions in all ages, and among all races, that dwell on the face of the earth. And they cried out aloud: "Oh, for some divine power to sunder the present from the past; to strip the human mind of its inherited trappings; to permit that mighty force, untrammelled intellect, to lead mankind forward into paths of peace and plenty and beauty forever!"

CHAPTER XXI.

THE FINANCIAL WORLD.

I HAVE, of course, in the last pages, anticipated somewhat the course of events.

It must not be supposed that amid the general rejoicing all men were happy. Far from it.

The capitalistic class, that class that desires to avoid the universal doom of work, by living on the crystallized and compounded labors of others, alive and dead, were thrown into a terrible panic. It really began to look as if they would have to do something to sustain themselves. It was an awful doom suspended over them—work! Their money was returned to them every day by the millions of dollars; it began to pile up in the banks in vast quantities; no one wanted it. The debtor class refused it, and the business classes were so tremendously prosperous that everything was upon a cash basis. What were they to do? To be sure, they could put their money into manufactures, or trade, and employ labor, and thus help the general prosperity. But this did not suit them. They would have to take the chances of the calamities and mishaps of life, and they had been so long accustomed to having some poor wretch stand between them and the contingencies of fortune, to take the brunt while they were in perfect security, that the alternative of coming down to the general level was dreadful to contemplate.

A great bitterness took possession of them.

Sophie was in New York city. She wrote me:

DEAR EPHE:—Be careful of yourself. A little while ago the capitalists of this city worshipped you. Now they hate you with the bitterness of death. You are ruining them in your efforts to help the people. In their desperation they will kill you to stop the outpouring of gold. Do not go anywhere without a guard. Be careful what you eat and drink.

I can see the change in my Woman's Aid Society. Several of the great ladies have refused to have anything further to do with it; and they are giving their trade to the sweating shops again. But we have progressed so far, and grown so strong, that we can get along without them. I cut the following clipping from the New York *Capitalist* of to-day:

"*Query:* Has any one man the right to destroy the entire wealthy class of this country, and derange the finances of the whole world? Is the life of any one man worth more than the business interests of the United States? These are pregnant questions which every man should consider and decide for himself. There are occasions when crime becomes a virtue. We have said enough."

And so I say again, my dear husband, guard yourself carefully against assassination. The meaning of that paragraph is very plain, and it is aimed at you.

I am hurrying up my work here, and will join you soon, to look after you. Affectionately your wife,

SOPHY.

CHAPTER XXII.

I ORGANIZE THE BROTHERHOOD OF JUSTICE.

I saw clearly the force of Sophie's suggestions. I knew there was nothing so desperate and cruel as human greed despoiled of its victims. You might just as well attempt to take the dead kid away from the famishing tigress, while her pups were clamoring at her dry dugs, as seek to wrest from robber man the wretches he was plundering. (There is more devil in man than in all the wild animals put together;) more of a cunning, complex, insatiable, unfathomable devil; wolf, tiger, fox, gorilla, lion, jackal—all stirred together in one horrible compound, with something of the demoniac from the external invisible world added thereto, which none of the hungry clamorers of the woods possesses—that is man! Animal brutality mixed with supernatural deviltry—that is man in his worst estate. And but for the better angels in human nature, it would be an improvement of the universe if God would blow up the planet, and shower its stony fragments on Mars and Venus; a drift age reminiscent of human depravity and the Creator's vengeance.

I saw that I could not rest the perpetuity of the

great work I was attempting upon the chances of my single life. I must form an association that would carry out my purposes, after I had passed away. I must form a corporation to which should descend all the vast wealth now loaned out by me, with the other hundreds of millions I intended to create. I did so. And I provided that, to prevent the assassination of all its members, and the destruction of the society, each member, the day he was appointed, should secretly designate three faithful men, whose names were to be preserved with such care that they could not be ascertained by the enemy; and if they came into office by the death of their principal, they were also, at once, to designate their three successors, whose names they should deposit in safe and secret keeping;—and so on from generation to generation. All these men were to be carefully selected for their intelligence, courage, education, and above all for their philanthropic spirit. Society has conspired against the existence of a benevolent breed of men, but there are enough left —God's inestimable gift to man—to save the world.

I called my society "The Brotherhood of Justice," for *justice* is, after all, a greater word than *liberty*. In fact, liberty is only protection from injustice. Justice means the equal balancing of man against man, without regard to the inequalities of capacity or fortune; it is the protection of one man's rights against all other men's power. Its emblems are the scales to weigh and the sword to strike. It assigns to each one his share, and defends him in the enjoy-

I ORGANIZE THE BROTHERHOOD OF JUSTICE.

ment of it. In the last analysis all good government simply *justice*. There can be no misgovernment that does not rob some man of his rights.

The first membership was confined to one dozen men selected by Mr. Hayes and myself, and one woman—Sophie. Sophie was vice-president; I was president, Mr. Hayes was secretary. In a great safe, under treble locks, was deposited the names of our successors.

Then we framed the constitution of the society. Its object was "to resist wrong and injustice." We guarded carefully against corruption. Each member was given a salary of five thousand dollars per year during his life-time. He was, therefore, under no inducement to betray his trust, as is too often the case, in order to provide for his old age. Even his wife and children were to receive a half-pay pension after his death, during their lives. Thus relieved of that great pressure of doubt and love, which too often makes even the virtuous vicious, the members could devote their whole lives and energies to the great work.

Then by proper legal conveyances I assigned to this corporation—this brotherhood—all the hundreds of millions of mortgages held by me; and by will I left them all other properties, real and personal, of which I should die possessed, after making liberal provisions for my wife, mother, and the other members of my family.

It was a great relief to my mind when all these

details had been attended to. I no longer feared death; for I knew the great work would go on, from generation to generation, with steadily increasing power. But Sophie, in her solicitude for me, told the newspaper reporters of the establishment of the Brotherhood of Justice, so that the wealthy class would understand that it would do no good to take my life, or the lives of all our members.

In addition to this corporation proper, in which the wealth was vested, we established lay memberships, which were open to all the people who sympathized with us in our work. We sent out agents into every state, county, and township; and the people, men and women, flocked into the society, and we soon numbered several millions of members.

Each member received free a copy of a great central organ, a weekly newspaper, *The Anti-Monopolist*, for which the best writers of the age contributed, and whose pages were illustrated by the greatest artists with pictures grave and gay. This journal started with one million copies, and within a year its circulation had reached over seven millions. Advertising space in such a paper was very valuable, and so graduated that it paid the whole cost of the journal, and we were able to distribute it freely to our members, and yet make it self-supporting. One highly intelligent and faithful man was employed to carefully read and collate brief extracts from the thousands of communications sent each week to the paper, and many excellent suggestions, of great use to mankind, were thus saved from oblivion; for it is a singular fact that nearly all new thoughts of value come from the common people. The multitude are the productive earth; the aristocracy are the air; it is the people that produces.

Editions of this great journal were printed in the different languages, and some were especially adapted to the farmers and others to the mechanics. Arrangements were also made to extend our society throughout Europe, so far as the jealous and suspicious governments would permit it; and whenever members joined in sufficient numbers, editions of *The Anti-Monopolist* were circulated in the different languages. I could thus reach, in a few hours, the minds and consciences of many millions of the best and most intelligent of the human race; and was thereby able to weld them together, into one mighty and effective whole. I thus possessed—

"The god-like power, the art Napoleon,
Of winning, moulding, welding, banding,
The minds of millions till they moved as one."

CHAPTER XXIII.

I START A TOWN AND BUILD A RAILROAD.

Our work had thus far helped principally the work-women and the farmers. But for the mass of the laborers, mechanics, artisans, in the cities, I had as yet done little. I could not lend them money to redeem their homes, for they very rarely had any. Nor could I advance them the means to buy homes in the great cities, for the prices of urban property was far beyond the reach of their humble means. The cities afforded splendid opportunities for the rich and the middle classes, but they presented no chance for the laboring men. They were driven to shiver or swelter in some garret or tenement house, or to spread themselves, in hot weather, upon the roofs of houses, panting to catch a breath of the devitalized air, while their children perished in the foul atmosphere, like mice under the glass ball of an air-pump. It is the doom of poverty to pay the highest prices for the poorest articles, and to be most lacking in those things which are the most essential to its comfort and happiness. It was labor that had made the cities, and yet labor was without respect in them. The workman's poorly paid toil had swelled the value of the city property far beyond his own reach. He was homeless by reason of his very industry.

What could be done?

This is how I solved the enigma.

I sent agents to quietly buy up vast tracts of land around Great Egg Harbor, on the sea-coast of New Jersey. This gave me a fine natural roadway for ships and a healthy site for a city.

Then, imitating Peter the Great, I took a map of the United States, and placed a ruler upon it, and drew a line from Great Egg Harbor to Philadelphia, and thence across the continent, straight as the crow flies, to the California coast at San Francisco, paying no attention to existing towns or cities.

Then I set shrewd agents at work in every legislature to quietly procure charters, or legislation, for local railroads, with electric motors, across the several States. They did this without exciting the suspicion of the great railroad interests, for no man could have foreshadowed my gigantic projects.

Then along this line at points about five miles apart I purchased thousands of acres of land for town-sites.

At the mouth of Great Egg Harbor River I erected an immense dam of stone, with a central doorway hundreds of feet wide; in this was a sliding gate of iron, which rose and fell automatically twice every twenty-four hours; and was so arranged that the top of the gate was always about a foot lower than the ocean tide at that time. In this way a great cataract of sea-water, hundreds of feet wide, poured over the top of the gate as the tide came in; and, shortly after high-tide, the gate began to fall automatically and the contents of the long river poured out again in the same way. From this salt-water Niagara I derived tremendous electric power; a small part of this was used to furnish the force requisite to slide the gate up and down, while the rest of it was to run the machinery in the mills and factories.

Then I laid out my city.

In the centre of the tract I drew a large circle. Here the electricity was conveyed for the use of the innumerable shops that were to be.

Every mile—north, south, and west—similar circles were laid out; they were also to be centres of manufacturing power.

Around these circles were parks or gardens, which insured fresh air and sunshine to the workers in the mills. Beyond the parks were the streets and lots of the city. There were two sets of streets—large avenues, stretching in successive circles around the manufacturing centres; and other wide avenues crossing these at right angles and centring where the mills and shops were to be erected.

Each lot was an acre in extent—each house was to stand in the midst of a garden.

Street-car lines, charging one cent for a fare, were provided for on all the avenues, and by a system of "transfers" one could pass to any part of the city without additional charge. The street-car lines were owned by the city.

I START A TOWN AND BUILD A RAILROAD. 167

Lots could only be held by persons actually residing on the same. Wherever a lot passed to a speculator or a tenant, it reverted, at once, to the government of the city, to be held, at the original price, five dollars, for the next man who would take it and live upon it. It was made the duty of the city government to lay out more lots, at the same price, as rapidly as the increase of population made it necessary. In this way no man could be without a home.

But as many of the working people were so poor that they could not build a house, I directed the construction of houses as fast as demanded. The cost of the lot and house was charged up in the tax roll, at two per cent per annum interest, and every year the interest and one-twentieth of the principal was collected with the other taxes.

I offered free power to all manufacturers who would build mills and factories, on condition that the work was to be conducted on the coöperative plan, each worker having a share of all the profits. I offered the same terms to combinations of the men themselves, with bank credit to enable them to carry on business. I established a bank of deposit and discount in every circle. In the very centre of each circle was erected a great town-hall, for the free use of those contiguous to it. Here were reading-rooms, lecture-rooms, art-schools, bath-rooms (supplied with sea-water), and shops where all necessaries could be bought at a small advance on first cost. Here, too, was a physician, paid by taxation, for every five thousand of population, free dispensaries of medicine, and a board of arbitration for the settlement of disputes free of cost to litigants.

Of course it required many months, and in fact years, to carry out all these plans; but as soon as it was known what was intended, the people began to swarm in by the thousands. Lines of boats soon presented themselves to carry passengers from New York, Boston, and all points on the sea-coast; and a branch railroad was built to New York and the main trunk line constructed to Philadelphia.

Every man who came wanted a home. The nest-building instinct is one of the strongest in humanity, but society has robbed its members of the opportunity. Thirty years ago the nation, after a hard battle, advanced, reluctantly, to the conception of a "Homestead Law;" that is, they gave each head of a family the right to take 160 acres of government land as a free gift, except the clerk's fees for making out the papers. And during the grasshopper times several state governments, in the West, had loaned money for food and seed to the suffering farmers; and it was quietly returned in a few years, into the State treasury, by the process of gradual taxation; and not a soul was a dollar worse off, while thousands had been enabled to live and save their homes. But no one had thought of applying these precedents to the case of the laboring people. The poor man is, at first, like the new-born child, he is perfectly powerless; he needs protection, if he would advance to the full stature of manhood. He has now fought his own way, by organization, a long distance; government must come to his help for the remainder of the path of progress he is to travel over.

When it became known that at "Coöperation," for so I called my new city, men could procure, not only homesteads, but *homes*—roofs to shelter wife and little ones from storms and heat and cold, the rush of applications was tremendous. We erected booths and tents on the sea-shore to temporarily cover them. It must have been a delight to the merciful angels of God to see the pale-faced, meagre, sickly children brought from the alleys and purlieus of the great cities, to expand in the sunshine and pure air into splendid rosy cherubs, as they played in the white sand, and the glorious salt winds tumbled their many-hued hair; for every head, in its complexion, told the long story of migrations of the human race, and the longer story of human miseries in the dark and dreadful past.

In rushed an army of mechanics; the harbor was alive with vessels loaded with lumber, lime, bricks, sand and stone; factories sprang up to make windows and doors and furniture. Thousands were at work laying out the streets, planting the gardens, erecting the houses, constructing the street-car lines. And every worker wanted a home. The men who were to build the railroads to New York and Philadelphia would not go out to work until they had first selected their lots and arranged for their houses.

And manufacturing capital which, without the aid of labor, was like a man without his hands and arms, finding that their employees had deserted the great cities, and knowing that they could procure electric power free of cost, came to Coöperation; they selected sites in the great circles, called the workmen together, and formed companies in which every man added the dignity of an employer to the profits of the toiler. There was no more oppression, for men do not oppress themselves; there were no more "strikes," for they could not "strike" against themselves; there was no more discontent, for each man understood the business conditions, and saw that he had a fair share in the general division. And the capitalist got a liberal return on his money and a just reward for his business capacity, and he found himself surrounded, not by enemies, but by a brotherhood of friends.

And the city grew. It arose with all the rapidity and splendor of a gorgeous dream. From every part of the world men poured in to share its far-heralded advantages. Labor was limited to eight hours a day, hoping that some day even this period would be shortened. There was not a drinking-place in the whole city; no man dispensed poison and slew his fellows for profit. The hours gained from toil were spent in the gardens, or with their families, or in the lecture-rooms, or in reading instructive books and newspapers in the reading-rooms, or in innocent sports and games. In every house was our great journal, and through it all our millions communed together,

I START A TOWN AND BUILD A RAILROAD. 171

and studied out what would make them better and happier.

And the stupid politicians, seeing all these results, scratched their wise heads and said to one another, "Why did not the State or the nation enter upon this great work long ago? Why does it now leave it to one man to do? Why did not the United States supplement the Homestead Law by a *Home* Law? Why did it not come with government loans to the help of the hundreds of thousands of farmers, who, during the last quarter of a century, were driven off the land by excessive rates of interest? Why did not the States stop the discontent of the working-people, ever ready to break out in civil war and endanger all social order, by using its power of 'eminent domain' to condemn and appropriate land for town sites, and its credit to borrow money to build homes for the people, to be repaid by gradual taxation, as this man has done? Why should not government expand its powers with the necessities of its surroundings? Has government any higher function than the relief of the human estate? And does not earthly power seem likest God's when it lifts up man and makes him contented, virtuous, and happy?"

In three years Coöperation contained half a million people. It was amusing to see how the speculators tried to get their claws on some part of this wonderful growth; and how we rapped them over the knuckles until they gnashed their teeth and howled with rage.

And then we began to develop, all along the line

of our trunk and branch railroads, other towns and cities on the same plan, with like results. We put rates of travel down to one cent per mile, and the trains had to run every quarter of an hour. And rates of transportation were reduced in like proportion, and we broke the back of the Pools, and squeezed all the water out of the railroad stocks, and the savings were divided between the farmers and the rest of the people. Our great four-track trunk line across the continent, with its north and south branches, could not do the business that crowded upon it; and Jay Gould went out and hung himself. And all the people said—Amen!

And the joy of the multitude was unbounded, and again the politicians asked, "Why did not the nation do all this long ago?" And echo—it was an Irish echo—answered, "because of the politicians."

CHAPTER XXIV.

THE DEMONETIZATION OF GOLD.

But I am ahead of my story.
Were the so-called Plutocrats idle?
Not at all.

There was a buzzing like that of an overturned bee-hive. The golden honey was on the ground, and the bees, with hot business-ends, were flying hither and thither seeking for revenge.

And Threadneedle Street and Lombard Street were as wildly excited as Wall Street.

They had educated the people for centuries in the worship of gold; they had crowned the yellow demon master of the souls and bodies of men; all wealth was prostrated before this Baal, humbly cringing and crawling on the ground. And now, as if by a jest of the Almighty, a boundless sea of gold was pouring forth and flooding the world. The purchasing power of money was decreasing rapidly, and the value of all forms of property, as well as human labor, was rising with equal rapidity.

Mankind was slipping between the fingers of capital!
The human race was attaining freedom.

An incident of commerce was no longer master of earthly destinies.

GOLD WAS A DRUG AND MONEY POWERLESS!

Long and earnestly did the Plutocrats counsel together.

To kill me was not a remedy; for they knew a vast society would live after me, possessed of enormous wealth, and probably the heirs of my great secret. A dozen men might then be making gold instead of one.

At last one long-headed man proposed a remedy.

"Gentlemen," said he, "you remember that when the Comstock lode began to pour out such vast quantities of silver, while the production of gold was annually decreasing, we agreed that, to preserve our supremacy, we must demonetize the abundant metal and make the scarcer metal the sole basis of the world's business. By arts which I need not more than refer to, we persuaded many nations, including this republic, to demonetize silver and establish a mono-metallic currency. The experiment worked admirably. The value of all forms of human property, food, clothes, implements, ornaments, bread, meat, and even the price of labor, fell off one-third, which signified one-third added to our wealth from the pockets of the multitude who created the wealth; we increased the value of the mortgage by reducing the value of the farm; we added to the value of the national bond and the individual indebtedness, by lowering the price of all things that could be sold to pay them, or the interest on them. The work would have gone on indefinitely, for the courts of Europe and the politicians of this country were, alike, our bond-slaves; and eventually we should have concentrated in our hands the great bulk of the possessions of the world. But in an unfortunate hour this pleasant boor of Kansas stumbled, in some mysterious and inexplicable way, upon the secret which the alchemists sought in vain for centuries, and which we fondly thought was securely hidden forever from the prying eyes of man. Now, then, we must meet the altered conditions by *remonetizing silver and demonetizing gold!*"

A look of astonishment passed over the faces of his auditors, but it quickly gave way to a smile of delight, and they broke forth into rapturous cheers; then they rushed forward and grasped his hand.

He had solved the problem!

Mankind had not yet escaped from the clutches of Plutocracy.

And immediately they set to work, busy as bees, to arrange the details.

The next day every daily paper in the United States contained articles demanding the demonetization of gold and the remonetization of silver, on high moral grounds; with many lucid arguments, showing that thereby the public would be greatly enriched and benefited! A few days subsequently all the weekly papers, except the Reform press, echoed the cry. In two weeks several million intelligent American citizens were clamoring for the demonetization of gold and the remonetization of silver, with a dim belief that they had been in favor of the same things for ten years past. It is extraordinary how rapidly our people take up the ideas of the newspapers. The public mind seems to be a *tabula rasa*, ready to receive the last impress of the type. No man in this country ever remembers what a newspaper said last week, any more than he can foresee what it will say next week; and as to any consistency between utterances a month apart, only an idiot would expect that. The mental appetite must have provender, and the newspaper restaurant furnishes it; and men eat with a divine faith, careless whether it be a stall-fed tenderloin or a round from the extremity of an omnibus mule. The rule is swallow, smile, and ask no questions.

In three weeks the whole people, with the exception of the readers of *The Anti-Monopolist*, and that small proportion who think for themselves, were howling for the remonetization of silver and the demonetization of gold.

This, however, was merely preparatory; a sort of greasing the wheels before corruption whipped up the horses of the chariot of government.

All the Washington lobbyists were summoned to New York.

In three weeks the House passed a bill to remonetize silver, to deny the legal-tender power to gold, and to shut the doors of the United States mints in the face of the royal yellow metal; and all the fools in the nation, and they constitute a large majority of

THE DEMONETIZATION OF GOLD. 177

the whole people, hurrahed until they split their throats.

I was in despair.

Sophie came to my help.

She advised me to corrupt the corrupters.

The bill had yet to pass the Senate. More than half the votes were already bought, but not paid for, to pass it.

Brooks held a conference with the lobbyists. He asked them frankly how much Wall Street had given them to buy up Congress. They told him, for they knew they were dealing with the agent of "the gold maker." Brooks offered them twice as much to kill the bill in the Senate. They agreed to do it. Wall Street never suspected the fidelity of its agents. Those worthies filled their pockets from both sides; they were paid to corrupt, and paid not to corrupt. The Senate voted down the bill unanimously. The Senators were astonished that they had remained virtuous and had voted with the people; and I was surprised that so great a danger had been so easily averted.

If the bill had passed the Senate, my power would have been gone. Gold would not have been worth ten cents on the dollar. It would, indeed, have had as much value as the cement and alloys which are used to fill decayed teeth, and no more. No woman would have cared to wear ornaments made of a metal cheaper than lead. The prehistoric superstition would have been deader than the sun-god Apollo. The last remnant of sun-worship would have disappeared from human society.

But I perceived the ticklish ground on which I stood.

It is true I did not believe in gold myself, but if the gullible world did not continue to believe in it, I could not effect the reforms which I had planned.

And so the next day I sent a circular letter to each United States Senator, in which I said that I believed their pay of five thousand dollars per year was totally inadequate to the demands, social and political, which were made upon them; that I did not believe in "muzzling the ox that treadeth out the corn;" that it "was hard for an empty sack to stand upright;" that it was unreasonable to place Aladdin in the garden of jewels, and not expect him to fill his pockets; that the administrators of hundreds of millions should be placed above the pressure of temptation, and much more of the same sort; and that I had, therefore, resolved to give to each one of them, during his term of office, ten thousand dollars a year extra, with five thousand dollars a year after the close of his term as long as he lived, and half as much to his wife if she survived him, only conditioned that they always voted on the side of the people.

The effect of this was magical. A majority of those Senators were naturally honest men, with a strong sense of the dignity of their position, and of their duty to the people who had sent them there.

But against these sentiments was the terrible pressure

for money to maintain their state and secure re-election; and the more terrible thought that they might be perfectly honest during their six years, and resist all temptations, and then die in the almshouses, or live in their old age objects of charity to relatives or friends. And so they had heretofore sold themselves, and their country, through what they esteemed the highest wisdom and the profoundest worldly prudence.

But when they found that income enough was insured them as long as they lived, and that their families were to be provided for, all that was good in their natures rose to the surface, and they began to labor to leave behind them great and honored memories, as true statesmen and benefactors of their race.

There were some who did not need these incitements to honesty, and there were others who were like monkeys, and stole by instinct, and would have purloined fence-rails if they had owned the planet. But I had erected a bulwark against corruption, and I had done it openly, without yielding a particle to the prevailing evil; for while I was ready to buy lobbyists, I would not corrupt legislators.

But there are no words to express the unbounded wrath of Wall Street. The New York daily papers were one continual scream of impotent rage. They were full of caricatures in which awe of my power was curiously blended with hate of my person.

An attempt was made to blow up my residence with dynamite in the middle of the night. Fortunately Sophie and I were at our secret place of abode, but the front of the house was largely destroyed, every window smashed for a mile in every direction.

There was a great uproar in the newspapers, and public sympathy was largely on my side.

I moved into another house and established triple rows of guards.

CHAPTER XXV.

I AM ELECTED PRESIDENT.

The election of a president was at hand.

The People's Party nominated me for the presidency. The subsequent rush of politicians was awful.

They wanted a barrel—no, not a barrel, a hogshead! Nay, a hundred hogsheads! A rich man buys not only by his money, but by the reputation that he has the money. Men bow to the sceptre even before it is wielded.

The Democratic National Convention met. There was a tremendous battle between Wall Street and the railroads on the one side, and the active politicians and the progressive young men on the other. The Monopolists poured out their wealth like water. I refused to pay a cent. I should have been beaten out of sight, but that an adventurous Missourian, without authority from any one, pledged vast sums of money to all who would vote for me. He carried the day; then he repudiated his promises, and asked for a place in the cabinet!

The Republican National Convention met. They had to appoint special police to keep the peace among the delegates; each side tried to howl the other down; they tore up each other's banners; pounded each other over the heads with the flag-staffs, and yelled and screamed like a pack of Comanche lunatics. This is what they called a "deliberative assembly," and the "force of public opinion." The chairman sold out both factions and was applauded equally by both. The four walls of the immense convention hall were lined with bars, and the bar-tenders stood three feet apart, behind barricades of bottles; and liquor enough flowed to have floated the American navy—which isn't saying much, either.

The battle was between the Plutocrats who wanted to defeat me, and the politicians who wanted the offices, and it was a terrible one.

At last Flanagan of Texas mounted the shoulders of a big fellow from Arkansas, and standing upright made a speech which settled the matter.

"What are we here for?" shrieked Mr. Flanagan. "Don't you d—d fools know that this isn't a question of principle, but of success? Are you asses enough to want to buck agin a man who can put ten million dollars into the campaign fund every ten minutes? Think of it! *Ten million dollars every ten minutes!* O LORD!"

The thousands of eyes that were uplifted to the speaker grew moist at the words, and their mouths drooled; and with an unearthly and overwhelming yell, the Republican National Convention indorsed my nomination for the presidency, and smashed the portraits of all the other candidates amid howls of savage execration.

The next day the national committees of the Democratic and Republican parties bolted! They met in every State in the Union and united to form a new party—a gold-bug party, to defend vested rights and special privileges; to remonetize silver and demonetize gold. They also demanded, as my transcontinental railroad had smashed the profits out of all the other railroads, that the nation must purchase and own at once all the railroads. They wanted to sell the government something that was now worthless.

It was enough to make one's head swim to see the men who had but lately been denouncing silver and praising gold, wheel around and denounce gold and praise silver. And it was equally perplexing to behold statesmen who had declared government ownership of railroads to be communism while the corporations had the people by the throat, now organizing a new party to force the government to buy all the railroads, because the people had the corporations by the throat. I was reminded of Abraham Lincoln's story of the two drunken men who got into a fight with their overcoats on, and they rolled and tumbled until each man had fought himself out of his own overcoat and into the overcoat of the other fellow.

But the moment the local committees of the two old organizations united the spell of party superstition was broken and their followers fled from them in swarms. They dissolved until there was nothing left of the two armies but the brigadier-generals. The fellows with the muskets and knapsacks had all trudged off into the People's Party camp.

I was elected by an overwhelming vote.

CHAPTER XXVI.

A CIVIL WAR PROBABLE.

I AM sorry to say Wall Street did not accept the results of the election with anything like the satisfaction it gave Sophie. In fact, they would not accept them at all.

After having spent millions of dollars in fruitless efforts to buy up the voters to vote against me, they now declared that I had corrupted the ballot-boxes, and that the election was void.

Leading financiers from London, Paris, and Berlin came over and counselled with them, for the gold I was pouring out was smashing things all over Europe.

Their first step was to corrupt the worthy man who then held the office of President of the United States. A few hundred thousand dollars made him all right. He agreed to hold on and use the army of the United States, if necessary, to keep me out of the presidential office.

Then they proceeded to quietly buy up enough electors to turn the scale by casting their votes for the candidates of the new gold-bug party.

In the mean time, the New York newspapers, and

all the journals that followed after them, were fairly blazing with daily appeals to the passions of the multitude.

The plan was to capture the forms of government, and put the people in the attitude of rebels against constituted authority. Then, without exposing their precious carcasses to danger or their pockets to loss, they would organize armies, to be paid by national taxation, to shoot down the voters. If the Republic perished in the struggle and a despotism was established, so much the better.

The people of New York City, by the unanimous and continual outcries of the daily press, had come to regard me as a destructive demon, and were ready to risk their lives to destroy me—indeed, companies, regiments, and brigades were already organized and equipped by the contributions of the Plutocracy; daily drillings took place with Gatling guns and rifles; and all the pride, pomp, and circumstance of glorious war was invoked against me.

I was in great perplexity.

What could I do? If I raised an army I should appear as a rebel, and I would have to fight the whole power of the Federal government, backed up, if necessary, by foreign nations. If I stood still, the cunning enemy would weave their nets of corruption about me, and sooner or later the conflict would have to come.

In this dilemma, my good angel—Sophie—as usual, came to my rescue.

"Who owns these newspapers that are tarring on the people to war?" she asked.

"Why," said I, "they are owned by joint stock companies, made up of many different stockholders."

"Is the stock for sale?" she inquired.

"Yes," I said, "it could be picked up on the market, I have no doubt. But what are you trying to get at?"

"What is to prevent you, with your boundless wealth," she asked, "from sending an agent to New York to quietly buy up, through brokers, a majority of the stock of each of the leading newspapers?"

I sprang up with delight.

"Precisely so," I cried, "a splendid idea! Controlling the stock, we would control the utterances of the papers, and controlling these we would control the opinions of the people. The Plutocrats would be disarmed. They could no longer lash the masses to white heat and get them to fight for them; they would not fight for themselves, and the whole rebellion would collapse. A splendid plan!"

"But," she said, "you must proceed with great caution. If the enemy surmised your plans, they would soon secure control of the stock. Not a whisper must be uttered to alarm them until everything is secure. Who can you send to New York?"

"Brooks?" I asked.

"No," she replied, "he is too well known. It must be some one that has no apparent connection with you."

"Then let us advise with Brooks," I said; "he is perfectly trustworthy."

Brooks suggested the name of one of his deputies—a Mr. Morton—a reliable, discreet, elderly man, who looked the capitalist to the life.

Mr. Morton was sent for, and we explained just what he was to do. A very large sum was delivered to him in cash, for drafts might be traced, and arrangements were made to forward him additional sums by express as they were needed.

Mr. Morton took his departure at once for New York.

CHAPTER XXVII.

HOW THE WAR WAS AVERTED.

When Mr. Morton reached New York he proceeded quietly, under the character of a wealthy gentleman seeking investments, to buy up, through two or three active brokers, all manner of securities, railroad stocks, bank stocks, manufacturing stocks, and newspaper stocks. The latter he retained, the others he quietly sold again in a few days through other brokers, as if he was speculating in them. Thus, day after day, he secured blocks of stocks in the leading newspaper corporations. He had agents out hunting them up in all directions, but always he purchased quantities of other stocks with them, in order to avoid suspicion.

In two weeks Brooks brought me this telegram:

"It is finished.
"Morton."

Sophie and I had been in daily consultation about this important business, and when Morton's dispatch announced that the trap was ready to be sprung, Sophie insisted that she must go to New York and spring it, and have the satisfaction of humbling the wretches who had so abused and denounced her good husband. I could not refuse her that gratification.

The next day the general manager of the *New York Thunderer* received a polite note from a leading member of the stock exchange, asking him to be kind enough to step to his office, a few blocks distant, to meet a lady, Mrs. Sophie Benezet, the wife of the President-elect, on some business of great importance to himself and his journal.

In a little while the general manager was shown into the back office, where Sophie, Brooks, and Mr. Morton awaited him.

"Mr. Newhall," said Mr. Morton, after the preliminary introductions, "may I ask what is the total amount of the stock of your corporation?"

"It is two million seven hundred and fifty thousand dollars," replied Mr. Newhall.

"Then one million three hundred and seventy-six thousand dollars would constitute a majority of that stock?"

"Certainly."

"Now, Mr. Newhall," said Mr. Morton, untying a package, "please examine these certificates of stock, and, after making sure that they are *bona fide*, please see how much they amount to."

The general manager of the *Thunderer* was by this time deeply interested. He examined the certificates critically.

"Are they all right?" asked Morton.

"Perfectly so," was the reply.

"How much do they amount to?" inquired Morton.

"Exactly one million five hundred thousand dollars."

"Precisely. You will see that they are all assigned to me, Zebulon Morton."

"Yes."

"Then I am the owner of the *Daily Thunderer*."

"Undoubtedly," replied Mr. Newhall, rather pale and very much excited.

"Is it necessary for me to call a meeting and elect new officers, or will you accept my orders?"

"That is but a form. You own the paper and have a right to control it in every particular. My resignation of the office of general manager is at your service."

"I do not want it. You will please continue in your place. It will rest with the Lady President to say whether any changes will be made in the employees of the paper."

Here Sophie spoke:

"Mr. Newhall, who has been writing the leading editorials of your paper for the last month, in which my husband has been so savagely assailed?"

"They are nearly all from the pen of Mr. Joseph A. Whitlock, a recent graduate of Yale College."

"Is he an enemy of my husband?"

"Not at all. He admires him—and he greatly admires—permit me to say—his wife," and Mr. Newhall bowed respectfully to Sophie.

"Why, then, does he assail him so violently."

"That, my dear madam," said Mr. Newhall, "was simply the policy of the paper. The stockholders desired it. Whitlock would have abused his mother in the same way, if he had received orders to that effect from me."

"Horrible! horrible!" said Sophie, "that a man should place education, culture, talent, at the service of another, to the surrender of conscience. It is the lowest possible species of mental prostitution. Why, this man, while admiring my husband and myself, would have lashed the populace into a frenzy to hang us both, and have justified the act."

"Oh, no, madam," replied Mr. Newhall, "you do him injustice. As soon as you were hanged he would have denounced the act, and helped to bring the guilty parties to justice. And he would probably have written very handsome obituary notices of both of you."

"In other words," said Sophie, "this college graduate, after exciting the mob to kill two worthy people, whom he admired, would then insist that the mob should itself be hanged for doing his work?"

"Precisely. You, of course, desire me to dismiss Mr. Whitlock. I shall do so at once."

"Not at all," replied Sophie, "let him keep his place. It is impossible to feel anything but utter and absolute contempt for such superserviceable virulence. Cleopatra might just as well have felt incensed at the asp for stinging her. Give him this paper and tell him if he can turn the torrent of his savage denunciation, day after day, along the lines herein indicated, he can sit in the editorial chair to the end of his days, distilling poison. Good-day, sir. Be good enough to say nothing of the change of ownership of the paper to any one outside of the office."

And Mr. Newhall bowed himself out, to convey to the official force of the *Thunderer* the startling information that the paper was now owned by "the goldmaker," the President-elect.

Mr. Whitlock, a gaunt, cadaverous, sickly-looking youth, received his instructions from Mr. Newhall, read the memoranda made by Sophie, lit a fresh pipe of tobacco, and, without a blush or a single sensation of abasement, proceeded to exude from his mental venom-bag an article that would astonish all New York on the morrow.

And all day long Sophie, Brooks, and Morton received one general manager after another, and went through the same formula of exhibiting the certificates of stock, and dismissing them, with the same directions and injunctions as to temporary secrecy.

CHAPTER XXVIII.

PLUTOCRACY PARALYZED.

The next morning the thunder roared and the lightning flashed out of a clear sky around the whole heavens.

To fully realize the change of front, let us take a leading editorial of the *Thunderer* the day before and another of the day after Mr. Newhall's interview with Sophie:

THE DAY BEFORE.

The evidences multiply that the free people of this country are not willing to submit patiently to the corrupt domination of that ignorant and brutal peasant barbarian of Kansas, who by some accident (for the fellow has not the first element of scientific acquirement in his composition) has discovered the art of transmuting the baser metals into something that looks like gold; we say *looks* like gold, for in the judgment of experts, it is simply an imitation of that metal. By squandering this counterfeited compound broadcast he has corrupted the ballot-boxes, and obtained a seeming claim upon the presidency; but the very electors he has bought up have become disgusted with the part they are expected to play, and refuse, like good citizens, to cast their votes for their dishonored candidate; and all the schemes of the daring demagogue are likely to fall to the ground.

It is impossible to enumerate the evils this man and his wife—a fit companion, whom he married out of a prison—

have inflicted upon the people of this country. Hundreds and thousands of clothing manufacturers have been forced to suspend business or go into bankruptcy. In this city thousands of houses, and tens of thousands of tenement-rooms stand empty, to the great injury of all business. The widows and orphans who have been brought to poverty by the confiscation of their railroad stock—"watered stock" this wretch called it—are innumerable; their name is legion. Millions of people have been gathered into the cities he has established along his railroads, and the day is near at hand when this South Sea bubble will break, and they will be left penniless. Our banking houses are overloaded with vast deposits of gold, silver, and paper money, for which there are no applicants; and many thousands of cultured men and women look forward with horror to the prospect before them: a future in which they will have to employ their wealth in the vicissitudes of trade and manufactures, or starve!

A thousand Judas Iscariots, ten thousand Benedict Arnolds, could not have effected the evil which this Kansas boor has accomplished in a few short years. And now he seeks to take possession of the presidency, and wield the whole power of the national government for the further working out of his terrible plans. The superstitious will see in this Alaric, this Attila, this Tamburlaine, a visible intervention of Satan in the affairs of the world, for the destruction of mankind.

Let the people organize. It is better that the people should die, baked in their own blood, than tamely and peacefully submit to this monster.

THE DAY AFTER.

There is no doubt that a conspiracy has been organized among the bankers and moneyed corporations of this country to plunge our whole land into civil war.

The *Thunderer* has repeatedly sounded a note of warning of the dangers into which we are drifting.

The Plutocracy has sent its agents to some of the electors, who were chosen by the people of the different States, to vote for that great statesman and philanthropist, the Honorable Ephraim Benezet, of Kansas, for President of the United States; and have bought them up to vote against him; in the hope that, amid the uproar and confusion that would follow, the liberties of the Republic might be forever destroyed, and an empire established upon the ruins of liberty, of which Plutocracy would be the corner-stone. A number of our corrupt contemporaries, we are sorry to say, have been willingly lending themselves to this damnable conspiracy, and have been inciting the people to arm themselves and prepare for war. John A. Jenkins, President of the First Nationalist Bank; William Smithers, President of the Chemicalistic Bank; Thomas Burke, President of the Androscoggin & South Shore Railroad Company, and Henry Arbuthnot, of the Transcontinental Electric Line, are the chief leaders in this desperate and diabolical game of treason and rebellion. If there is any blood to be shed, let it be the blood of these men (their residences can be found in the directory), who are inciting the mob to murder the greatest benefactor of the human race that has appeared since the time of Socrates.

By his powerful genius Ephraim Benezet has solved the problem which has occupied the minds of the greatest of mankind for a thousand years—the transmutation of the baser metals into gold. And instead of using this tremendous power for his own gratification or aggrandizement, he has employed it to make millions happy. His lovely spouse, whom to know is to admire and honor, has lifted up the status of womanhood in this whole land, and brought joy to a million hearts of poor working women. Home is rendered safe, virtue triumphant through her great and humane labors. The President-elect, by his loans to the mortgaged multitude, at two per cent per annum, has broken the back of the money-lending oligarchy, and given the country the tremendous prosperity which it now enjoys. By the building of the great city of Coöperation, he has shown how the poorest workingman can procure, for a mere pittance, a home which thousands of dollars would not buy in a city of the same population. While, on the other hand, his great transcontinental railroad has reduced the cost of transportation of persons and property enormously; has increased travel and intercourse among the people, and has literally blotted out seven billion dollars of "watered stock," which was drawing nearly five hundred million dollars' interest annually out of the pockets of industry.

It is for these vast works of public beneficence that Jenkins, Smithers, Burke, Arbuthnot, and their wicked associates hate him, and have sought to create a civil war and deluge the land in fraternal blood; they know very well that if Ephraim Benezet goes into the White House, he will use his additional powers for the good of the human race, and the increased prosperity of every man and woman on earth.

No words can be too strong to apply to these desperate miscreants who, for a little personal profit, would wreck the whole world. We are surprised that the public has permitted them to so long pollute the atmosphere of this fair city with their presence. They should be strung up to the nearest lamp-posts.

Every other daily paper in New York City contained similar articles. There was only one editor who refused to change front in twenty-four hours in this shameful way. I have forgotten his name. He resigned his place. But it was at once filled by another who urged the multitude to mob the houses of Jenkins and his associates.

There are no words that can paint the utter astonishment of the people of New York when they rose from their beds and read the morning papers. They had to peruse the editorials two and three times over to get the meaning into their inner consciousness. The old gentlemen rubbed their spectacles vigorously, and looked through the glasses carefully, as if they had been bewitched. The multitude began to gather and murmur, in knots, on the street corners. "It was all true," they said, "President Benezet had done a great work for the good of all of them; and yet some of them had been incited by the capitalists to mob and kill him, or to enlist and fight against him." No man thought of accusing the newspapers of inconsistency, any more than they would have complained of the fences, because they did not have the same showbills plastered over them to-day that they had yesterday. But the wrath against the bankers rose high.

And there was a great meeting of wealthy men in a large room on Broad Street, summoned by telephonic and telegraphic messages. Guards stood at the door. A committee was at once dispatched to inquire how and why the newspapers had dared to change front in that way. The committee returned in an hour or two, and reported that twenty millions of dollars had been invested by Ephraim Benezet in the stock of the principal journals, and that he now owned and controlled them all.

Awe fell upon the assemblage at this statement. They perceived that they were disarmed, powerless. Their tongues were plucked out. Their power to do evil was gone.

But the committee made a still more alarming statement: they reported that mobs were gathering in every part of the city, full of imprecations and threats of death against the rich men of the city.

The meeting dissolved as if by magic, and every man made for the nearest railroad station, leaving his wife and children to the chances of the mobs. It is true they sent telegraphic messages from the first station the trains stopped at, ordering their families to join them without a moment's delay at their country seats.

And so the civil war ended.

The bribed electors voted for me, with the money of the Plutocracy in their pockets; and everything was lovely; virtue was rewarded, and there was peace in the land.

CHAPTER XXIX.

MY INAUGURAL MESSAGE.

My popularity was greater than ever. Most of the newspapers of the country followed the lead of the New York editors, re-casting their ideas, as usual, into a variety of new forms. Those who liked me went into ecstasies. Those who did not praised Sophie. For Sophie was altogether admirable.

Washington had never before seen such crowds as swarmed into it on the fourth of March, and during the previous week. The universal prosperity and the cheap railroad fares set every one to travelling. A man or woman could see the world for little more than it cost to stay at home. The poet says:

"Home-keeping youths have ever homely wits,"

and the people were glad to travel; the whole country swarmed with smiling happy faces, and life looked like a universal pic-nic. And the children! Even the mechanics' children were handsome, hearty, and well dressed; and in their gay colors they looked like a flower garden. In fact, you could scarcely tell the working-man and his family from the members of the mercantile class; shorter hours of labor and relief from a hundred oppressions had lifted them up into a contented, well-fed, well-clad people. The increase of mental activity consequent on increased prosperity was something astonishing. Every man and woman had a book or a newspaper. The pursuit of authorship became the most profitable in the country; any man who could instruct or entertain the multitude had his fortune made. The cars, the shops, the highways, and the by-ways rang with continual laughter. Men and women sang as they worked, and they worked with marvellous zeal, for every stroke of their muscles distilled money into their own pockets, and enjoyments into their own souls. Even the aristocracy, when they found that no one would borrow their dollars and become their bond-slaves, entered into various business enterprises on their own account, and the universal prosperity carried them forward to greater wealth. And the churches swarmed—not with women alone, but with sturdy men, who thanked God because they had something more than mere life, painful and perplexed, to thank Him for. They thanked Him for the glory of the world and the beauty of justice, fair play, and freedom, and the delights of loving one another. And the preachers forgot the past to preach about the present. They realized that God not only *was* but *is;* and that the best way to worship the Creator is to make his creatures happy. And dogmas disappeared in deeds. And Christ came out of the dark and brutal and barbarous past, which murdered him, and walked triumphant through the hearts of millions of happy, laughing, cultured people who loved him. Oh, it was a world worth living in!

And upon these matters I dwelt in my inaugural message.

I pointed out that there was but one thing that prevented our nation from rising to still higher levels of greatness and happiness—that was, the Old World.

"America," I said, "was united by a ligament to a corpse—Europe! [Sensation.] Decay and death spread along the tides of commercial intercourse from the rotten to the living. Every oppression practised beyond the Atlantic was represented by the degradation of labor in America. [Cheers.] Our politics had been distorted for nearly a century by attempts to fence out, by tariff legislation, the goods made by the pauper-labor of Europe. But when we had fenced out the goods made by the oppressed laborers of the Old World, the laborers themselves swarmed to our shores in such numbers, and in such depths of desperate wretchedness, that they were used by the capitalists to break down the wages of the American workmen. [Cheers.] Hence followed a persistent demand for legislation to close the portals of the continent against the wretched victims of Old-World injustice and despotism,

"'To shut the gates of mercy on mankind.'

"We could, by wise laws and just conditions, lift

up the toilers of our own country to the level of the middle classes, but a vast multitude of the miserable of other lands clung to their skirts and dragged them down. Our country was the safety-valve which permitted the discontent of the Old World to escape. If that vent was closed, every throne in Europe would be blown up in twenty years. [Great cheers.] For the people of the Old World, having to choose between death by starvation and resistance to tyrants, would turn upon their oppressors and tear them to pieces. [Immense applause.]

"Europe to-day is an armed camp built on the prostrate bodies of the producers. [Cheers.] Every man in the Old World who toiled worked with a scowl on his face and a bayonet at his throat. [Applause.] Every worker carried a soldier on his back, who reached down and took the bread out of his platter. [Great cheers.]

"The new civilization must extend a helping hand to the old. The whole moral influence of this giant republic must be thrown upon the side of the people in their struggles with kingcraft. [Long-continued applause, several times renewed.] We must withdraw our ministers from every kingdom and empire in Europe, to emphasize our detestation of systems of government which make paupers of the producers of all wealth, and drive those paupers across the Atlantic to break down our own prosperity. [The whole vast audience, acres in extent, screamed for ten minutes their approbation of these sentiments.]

"I do not say we should wage war upon the kingdoms of the Old World, and carry the stars and stripes on a crusade of liberty [cheers]; but I do say we should give the people of the Old World to understand, that they are horribly misgoverned; that our sympathies are with them; and that it is better that one-half of one generation should perish in their own heart's blood, if thereby all subsequent generations can be lifted up out of inexpressible misery. [Immense cheering.]

"What! Are we to sit still, with cowardly selfishness, and see wrong and inhumanity triumphant and utter no word against it. [Cries of "No, no."] Is the mighty republic to stand trembling before the tinsel thrones and the pasteboard crowns, and the insolvent brutes and debauchees who wear them? [Tremendous applause.] No, no; our flag bears stars of hopes for all the world, and its stripes are stripes of blood for the oppressors of humanity. [Great cheering.] God Almighty did not intend that the fulminations of the Declaration of Independence should be bounded on the east by the Atlantic Ocean and on the west by the Pacific Ocean. [Cheers.] The planet is not big enough for truth—the doctrines of the Revolution of 1776 will yet extend over all the continents and all the islands of the sea. [Great applause.] There can be no peace so long as a single toiler is denied the fruits of his own industry. [Thundering cheers.] For the first time, the great republic cries out to the humble of all the world:

'The blessings we enjoy should be yours; it is better to die fighting than live slaves.' "

It is impossible to describe the enthusiasm of the people. The air was white with handkerchiefs; the women cried. America had spoken through her chief magistrate, and his voice rang like a trumpet peal over all the world.

But Wall Street gnashed its teeth and tore its hair. Everything was going to destruction. The devil had broken loose.

CHAPTER XXX.

EUROPE PREPARES FOR WAR.

The London *Times* came out the next day in a double-leaded leading editorial headed, "To your Tents, O Israel!"

It said:

A madman has been elevated to the Presidency of the United States.

Filled with the fanaticism of that terrible people—the most daring, energetic, and warlike in the world—he has proclaimed destruction to the most cherished and venerable institutions of England and Europe.

The "universal war of opinion," so long prophesied by seers and statesmen, is at hand.

The oceanic republic is about to overflow its dykes and flood the world.

The first step taken by this fearful man was to pour forth gold in unheard-of quantities, and thus unsettle the business of all nations, and shake the social system to its very foundations. Already a vast unrest pervades all classes on this side of the Atlantic. Men are questioning all things that do not make for their individual happiness. Creeds, doctrines, time-honored beliefs are all being cast into the furnace. Nothing is sacred but what these fanatics call "humanity." The old theory that the inequalities of society were established by God, and that the miseries of the multitude were foreordained by Divine Wisdom, and that seeming injustice here was to be made right in another existence elsewhere, all these sublime doctrines of the fathers have disappeared before a storm of sacrilegious hootings that fill the heavens.

It may already be too late to save society and order from universal rout and ruin.

Not a moment is to be lost. Unfortunately no one foresaw what this newly-chosen lunatic would say in his inaugural address, and the result is that the newsgatherers, acting automatically, have spread the poison of his words into every home in every country on the continent, except Russia. His utterances have fallen like sparks of fire in magazines of gunpowder; his voice rings over all the world like a cry "To arms!" No man can measure the injury already inflicted by this insane miscreant. All Europe is honeycombed by communistic ideas. The crust of social order is growing thinner every day, and beneath it is the molten, blazing sea of Anarchy. If the governments would save society, they must strike at once

Let England take the initiative. It resisted the bloody flood of the French Revolution a century ago, but now a greater danger is at hand. Mirabeau, Danton, Robespierre are all wrapped up in this western demagogue, Benezet; and France was but a province compared with the continental area and power of the great republic of America. Let the telegraph do the work of diplomacy. In the words of Macbeth—

......"From this hour,
The very firstlings of our heart must be
The firstlings of our hand."

In twenty-four hours England had declared war against the United States, backed up by all Europe, except the republics of Switzerland and France. Every army was mobilized, and the Old World was a swarming camp of soldiers.

The battle of the ages, between liberty and despotism, was at hand.

CHAPTER XXXI.

THE CONQUEST OF CANADA.

I ISSUED at once the following call for volunteers:

EXECUTIVE OFFICE, WASHINGTON, D.C.
TO THE PEOPLE OF THE UNITED STATES:—
All the despotisms of Europe are moving to attack us.
The nation needs two million men.
Our offence is that we are free, and that we dare speak in behalf of freedom.
The objects of attack are · first, the nation; secondly, the rights of man.
The shackles are already forged that are to chain our limbs.
The faithful sons of the republic must, at once, come to the rescue of their country.
Recruiting offices will be opened in very town and city.
Must liberty die on this western continent, or shall it spread over all the world?
What is your answer?

EPHRAIM BENEZET,
President of the United States.

In ten days two million men were enrolled. Old and young fought for the privilege of enlisting. This was America's answer to infuriated Europe.

In ten days more three hundred thousand men, many of them without uniforms and carrying hunting rifles, but all with the courage of lions, crossed into Canada at Niagara Falls.

THE CONQUEST OF CANADA.

The blow was so sudden that resistance was impossible.

Two-thirds of the force, under the command of General Weaver of Iowa, moved eastwardly with great rapidity and captured Ottawa. The remainder of the force, under General Field of Virginia, seized the Canadian Pacific Railroad, and in a few days they had taken possession of Winnipeg, and everything else between Lake Erie and Puget Sound. The French of Quebec refused to fight to maintain English domination, and the greater part of the English-speaking population had been hungering for "annexation" for years, and cheered the starry banner as it advanced into their provinces. In one month from the issue of my call for troops, Canada had fallen into our hands like a ripe pear.

It was not conquest. It was simply occupation.

General Norton of Illinois was left in charge of the forces in lower Canada, while General Ellington of Georgia assumed command of the rest of the country.

I issued a proclamation declaring the several provinces territories of the United States, with a view of future admission into the Union as sovereign States.

Recruiting offices were opened in all the Canadian cities, and hundreds of thousands of men, Irish, Scotch, English, Germans, French, volunteered for service under the stars and stripes. "One touch of liberty made the whole world kin."

CHAPTER XXXII.

THE CONQUEST OF IRELAND.

Mighty forces were concentrating in England, Germany, Austria, Russia, Spain, and Italy.

Attempts had been made to arm the people of the Scandinavian peninsula, but the liberty-loving Swedes, Norwegians, and Danes refused to make war against their kindred in America, and the rulers found that to force them would breed revolution.

It was proposed to invade the United States with five million men by way of Canada. But our swift occupation of that country put an end to the scheme. Then an attempt was made to draw Mexico into the conspiracy, and two of the principal ministers of Diaz were corrupted by foreign gold; but that great man found it out and incontinently hanged them. He then raised a large army and entered into a treaty, offensive and defensive, with the United States.

The United States was one universal workshop. The people entered into the war as they would into a holiday excursion. The whole coast was fortified at every assailable point, and all the bays, harbors, and river-mouths bristled with cannon, submarine vessels, and terrible explosives.

In the mean time I had not been idle. As soon as I saw that war was inevitable, I had ordered the construction of three hundred steamers, swift war-ships of large capacity. Immense numbers of men worked day and night upon them.

Half a million well-equipped soldiers, many of them gray-headed veterans of the Civil War, from both North and South—for the South was more zealous in the defence of the nation, if possible, than the North—were concentrated in Boston, New York, Philadelphia, Norfolk, and Charleston. Hither were sent five hundred steamers; every passenger steamer had been impressed for the work, and in addition I had levied upon all our war-ships, and at the same hour the work of embarkation began and proceeded rapidly. Sealed orders were given to the commanders, to be opened as soon as they left port, directing them to concentrate at that point in the ocean where the 35th degree of north latitude crossed the 60th degree of longitude west of Greenwich, and sail thence directly for the harbor of Queenstown, Ireland.

I established my headquarters on the great steamer the *John Adams of Massachusetts*. Sophie was with me. I tried to persuade her to remain behind, and represented to her all the dangers of the expedition; but she was insensible to fear, and I had to yield. She was determined to share all risks with me, and, as the event proved, she was ready to follow me to the cannon's mouth.

It was a lovely day in June when we sailed out

of New York harbor. The white sands of Long Island were alive with people, and gayly decorated pleasure-boats darted to and fro breathing delicious music. All cheered us, for, while they did not know our destination, they surmised that something important was about to be undertaken.

The sea was like glass when our large flotilla reached the trysting-place. The ships from Boston had already arrived, and the next day our entire squadron had safely concentrated, and we moved eastward, the grandest armada that had ever sailed the seas.

The ocean roughened a little as we approached the British Islands, but Providence, which had sent the tempests that overthrew King Philip the Second's slave-making expedition, stilled the winds in their caves, because He knew we carried with us the banner of liberation for mankind.

I had selected Cork, or Queenstown harbor, as our point of destination, because the whole south coast of Ireland is a mass of bays and indentations, and I knew that if repulsed at one point we could readily find a landing-place close at hand; and I selected Ireland in preference to England, because I knew if we once got ashore we would find ourselves in the midst of a friendly people, from whom we could raise large numbers of recruits; and with this in view, we had brought with us guns, ammunition, uniforms, etc., for two hundred thousand more soldiers.

I threw part of our force on shore to the west of

Carlisle Fort, and a sudden charge upon the astonished and bewildered defenders from the rear resulted in its capture. Similar tactics soon gave us Camden Fort, on the east side of the entrance to the outer harbor, and we were speedily in possession of safe anchorage, and the work of disembarkation commenced. The whole country turned out to look at the mighty apparition which had seemingly risen from the waves; but when they saw the "stars and stripes," and understood that the long prayed-for deliverers had arrived, sent by their kindred beyond the seas, their joy was unbounded. The hills, black with people, rang with cheers; bonfires were kindled where the beacon-lights shone in the ancient days; the telegraph flashed the joyful news to every part of the island; and the bold and adventurous people rose everywhere, arming themselves with scythes, clubs, and extemporized pikes, and singing the old song—

"Oh, the French are on the sea,
Says the Shan Van Vocht."

The English government was astounded. The aristocracy were not ready. They had hoped to have attacked the United States from Canada, but Canada was lost to them. Then they had planned to invade us through Mexico; but that expedient was out of the question. They then made up their minds to assail our long lines of seacoast with troops of the different nations belonging to the coalition, and land and wage a desolating war on our soil; but now, to their utter surprise, they found the battle-field of humanity had been transferred to their own territory; a territory swarming in every part with discontented and oppressed people, who hated the powers which had so long ruled and impoverished them.

But the government moved with its old promptitude. It collected its regular troops, over 100,000 strong, at Holyhead, for the invasion of Ireland, and gave orders to the 40,000 armed constabulary of the Green Island to concentrate at once and resist our advance. Then it made vigorous appeals to the English and Scotch people to volunteer in defence of their native land.

As rapidly as our troops landed, they were pushed forward.

The people rose in Cork and delivered up the city without a blow.

A considerable force under the command of General Vincent of Indiana advanced on Limerick, but long before they could reach it the gallant inhabitants, filled with the spirit of their ancestors, rose *en masse*, captured the constabulary and the soldiers in the barracks, and met the advancing Americans with the "harp and sun-burst" flying in the air in triumph.

All Tipperary and Kilkenny were in arms; the very women marched, carrying babies and pikes.

Recruiting offices were opened in every town as we poured forward, and strong men wept as the breech-loading Winchesters and the American uniforms were dealt out to them. I never witnessed such wild excitement as our starry banner produced wherever it appeared.

The 40,000 constabulary gave us no trouble; the people took care of them. I had issued orders to avoid the shedding of a single drop of blood if possible, and not a life was sacrificed. The whole population rose up, and the police dissolved into them and reappeared, cheering, with the American uniforms upon their limbs.

Wexford, Kerry, Clare, Queens, Wicklow, Kildare were ours, and the mountains of Galway were blazing with bonfires and enthusiasm; and with a rush we poured into Dublin, and the American flag was soon flying from the top of O'Connell's statue.

Even the Orangemen of the North would not fight against the stars and stripes; and although they gathered in sullen squads, with hostile intent, as our shining platoons came in sight with the bands playing, they cheered with the rest. It was the irresistable and universal contagion of Liberty.

In the principal towns I established shops for the manufacture of guns, ammunition, and cannon, and the whole male population between eighteen and fifty were enrolled as a national militia, called the *Fianna Eirionn*. The unemployed were set at work constructing fortifications along the seacoast and around the principal cities.

I issued the following proclamation:

IRELAND IS FREE!

After seven hundred years of bloodshed and bondage, the shackles are at last torn from her limbs. The unconquerable spirit of the people is now crystallized into a nationality. In the name of the free people of the United States of America, I decree the establishment of the Republic of Ireland.

On the 4th day of July the whole people will assemble in their respective parishes, and elect delegates, on the basis of one for every ten thousand of population, to assemble at Tara on the 12th day of October next, the anniversary of the day when Wolf Tone, in 1791, organized the first society of United Irishmen.

Every acre of land in Ireland having been many times confiscated, and all titles resting therefore on force, the entire soil of the country is now, by right of conquest, declared to belong to the United States of America, which will hold it in trust for the benefit of the inhabitants of the island. The entire country will be resurveyed, and a redistribution of the land made as rapidly as possible, and given to actual occupants, free of cost, under provisions similar to those of the Homestead Law of the United States. No person shall own or occupy with his family more than fifty acres; the present occupants shall have the right to select a portion not greater than that amount, which may embrace the buildings used as a residence, etc. Where those taking land are not able to build a house, one shall be erected for them, and the cost of it, with the price of a horse and cow and necessary subsistence for one year, shall be charged up to the settlers at two per cent per annum interest, and paid for in instalments, collectable as taxes during the next twenty years. Tenantry is forever abolished.

To carry on this and other necessary works, the provisional government shall issue "greenbacks," full legal-tender, for all debts, public and private, which shall be gradually increased until they have reached a maximum of fifty dollars *per capita*. No banks of issue shall ever be permitted in the island, but all money shall be created by the government.

The new Republic is based upon the following principles:
1. Universal education.
2. Universal and impartial suffrage.
3. Universal religious toleration.
4. Absolute and complete separation of Church and State.
5. Absolute freedom of elections, and secrecy of the ballot, secured by the Australian system.
6. Absolute equality of all persons before the law.
7. A graduated income tax that shall prevent the accumulation of enormous fortunes, by confiscating all above a reasonable sum.
8. Limitation of the amount of land that can, at any time in the future, be owned by any one person or corporation.
9. The punishment of official bribery by death; and the punishment of the bribery or intimidation of voters by imprisonment for life.
10. No person to vote, after the expiration of ten years, who cannot read and write.

Let there be peace. Gather from the past not wrath and revenge, but wisdom to avoid the evils of the future. The distinctions of race and creed are adventitious and accidental; men in their beliefs are what their parents were; in themselves they are what God made them. You are all one people, with characteristics that are the product of the same soil and climate. Your first duty is to make your nation great and prosperous, and each other happy. He who would divide you hates you. You fell into slavery, many centuries ago, by senseless internal divisions. See to it that you do not lose your new liberties in the same way. Be a band of brothers, and let the differences of dogma and race be forgotten. Assemble at the site of the ancient capital of your country, and form a government so wise, just, generous, and benevolent that it will forever make the name of Irishman glorious.

EPHRAIM BENEZET,
President of the United States and Commander-in-Chief of the Army of Liberation.

CHAPTER XXXIII.

ENGLAND'S SURPRISE.

THE English army was preparing to cross St. George's Channel. A vast fleet of ironclads and transports was swarming along the coast of Wales. Every available soldier was withdrawn from London and all the great cities, and the railroad lines were loaded down with men and munitions of war. The London dailies bristled with violent denunciations of the Yankees, and appeals to the patriotism of the people to rise to the defence of the great nation which had overthrown all invaders, since victory crowned the Bastard of Normandy on the bloody field of Hastings.

We made ready for a terrible conflict on the coast of Ireland. A railroad was built along the whole coast, and connecting lines formed so that we could concentrate our forces wherever the blow might fall.

I grieved over the prospect of bloodshed. I loved and honored the English people—for no race in the Old World had done more than they for the supremacy of law and the cause of freedom. I loved them for the sake of Francis Bacon, and Pym, and Hampden, and Chatham, and Gladstone, and all the innumerable patriots who had lived or died to advance the race. I believed with Holmes that—

> One-half her soil had walked the rest,
> In poets, statesmen, heroes, sages.

It was the English aristocracy that had afflicted the world, not the English people. That aristocracy had not oppressed Ireland and India any more cruelly than they had their own countrymen. The swarming countless millions, for whom life had been a hopeless hell, were and are the victims of that brutal selfishness which William the Norman had infused, as a dreadful inheritance, into English history. And his beastly body, falling to pieces with its own rottenness as it was lowered into the grave, amid the curses of those he had robbed, was a fit type and figure of the end of his own corrupt aristocracy.

But while the government of England was rallying its troops to cross the channel, a great revolution had been going on in the minds of the English people. The newspapers had informed them of our course in Ireland; of the fact that not one drop of blood had been shed in the conquest of the country; and that we had decreed the sequestration of all the land in the island, and its division among the people, with provisions to build every man a shelter for wife and little ones, and help him with provisions until he could harvest his first crop. They had read of the breaking up of the great parks of the aristocracy, kept as preserves for wild animals, for the amusement of a few rich people, into farms and homes for the poor children of God; and every laboring man had said to himself: "Why should not England have such a system of laws as that, and why should we fight and die to perpetuate a costly royal family and a greedy aristocracy, who will suck the blood out of our veins and the veins of our children, for all generations?"

And the more men talked of these things, the more excited they became. And, hearing of it, I issued a proclamation and sent it broadcast throughout Great Britain:

PEOPLE OF ENGLAND, SCOTLAND AND WALES

We come not to enslave but to liberate you!

The great United States of America have no desire to rob you of a penny of your possessions. In the fulness of time the burden of the nations has become greater than they can bear: God has heard your cries and sent you help. "The stone cut out of the mountain without hands" is about to fall upon the feet of the "great image made of iron and miry clay," (the iron of power and the clay of rottenness), and break them to pieces forever. For—

"None calleth for justice, nor any pleadeth for truth; they trust in vanity and speak lies; they conceive mischief and bring forth iniquity. They hatch cockatrice's eggs, and weave the spider's web; he that eateth of their eggs dieth; and that which is crushed breaketh out into a viper. Their feet run to evil, and they make haste to shed innocent blood; their thoughts are thoughts of iniquity, wasting and destruction are in their paths.

"Yea, truth faileth, and the Lord saw it, and it displeased him, that there was no judgment. And he saw there was no man, and he wondered there was no intercessors; therefore his arm hath brought forth salvation, and his righteousness sustained him."

Why should you heat the fire to weld your own shackles? Why should you die that the oppressor may live?

I proclaim the Republic of Great Britain.

Liberty, Equality, Fraternity!

Equal rights, equal privileges, equal opportunities, for all men and women.

The land for the people and people for the land. No more aristocracy; no more paupers. The whole power of God's tremendous natural world utilized, by all the capacities of the human mind, to give abundance, prosperity, peace, happiness, and culture to all men.

The clock of the centuries is striking even now in the halls of God :—" the century's aloe flowers to-day."

Shall puissant England tear the Nessus shirt of craft and cruelty from her manly limbs, and robe herself in the shining garments of freedom?

The eldest-born of her children crosses the blue ocean to bring her liberty and justice.

Meet at once and take council together and organize the Republic.

Done in the name of the United States of America.

EPHRAIM BENEZET,
President and Commander-in-Chief of the
Army of Liberation.

So greedy were the newspapers for news, that the wires carried this proclamation to every city, town, and hamlet of England and Scotland before the government could interfere. In one night it covered Great Britain. Surely God has prepared the way for great events when He has given, through man's inventive skill, the power to millions of men to think the same thought at the same instant.

Magical, indeed, was the effect of this appeal falling on soil already prepared for it during centuries.

Edmund Burke said that he knew of no way to draw an indictment against a whole people.

England knew no way to make war on her whole population; for in millions upon millions they had assembled everywhere, in vast masses, and demanded a change of government—reform.

The contagion spread like lightning to the troops assembled at Holyhead. A few officers, belonging to the upper classes, tried to stem the sweeping torrent of public opinion, but they were at once overwhelmed. The cry "America! America! America!" rang through the embattled hosts, with a roar like the thunder of old ocean as it bursts, storm-smitten, upon the rocky coasts of Albion. Everywhere among the troops, all over England and Scotland, the flag of the United States was improvised; sometimes they got the stars in the wrong corner, but what did that matter? Every one knew that the grand banner signified—stars or no stars—salvation for mankind, justice for the humblest, and triumph for the highest aspirations of the human soul. It had ceased to be the flag of a nation—it had become the banner of mankind.

England was not conquered. She had liberated herself. The grand, self-governing race had leaped at one bound to the full stature of freedom.

There were no conflicts. Even the nobility, as in the French revolution, were swept along in the mighty flood, and many of them came forward and renounced their titles, and declared that their order had outlived its usefulness and had degenerated, too often, into disgraceful bestiality and brutishness.

And the cry came over to me in Dublin:

"Come and help us!"

CHAPTER XXXIV.

RECONSTRUCTED GREAT BRITAIN.

MANY questions perplexed them.

Two feelings struggled in their hearts. They desired to preserve their general government, and yet each subdivision of the country demanded local self-government. The provisional authority ended the dispute by calling national conventions to meet at Ayr (Robert Burns' birthplace); St. Albans (Francis Bacon's home); and Monmouth (the birthplace of Henry V.). The people began to perceive that there was nothing greater in a free country than its great men. The provisional government suggested that the nations should arise out of the people, and then the nations could, if they saw fit, delegate certain limited powers to a general government; but always the great fountain of authority and reservoir of primal power was to remain in and with the people. Nothing that the voters could do themselves was taken out of their hands; hence the power of the parish or town-meeting was immensely increased; for with every remove from the people the danger of usurpation and misgovernment becomes greater.

I urged the provisional government to establish at

once a greenback currency for each nation, and to commence the work of surveying the land, building houses, draining swamps, constructing roads, manufacturing guns, etc., so as to give employment and food to the millions of poor but willing workers.

I then urged them to imitate our plans in the United States, and near every large city take possession of land and establish a new city, for the workingmen, where they could obtain homes forever at a nominal price, and escape from the power of the landlords. This they did with splendid results.

Some of the aristocracy complained bitterly about the destruction of their hunting parks; but the wiser ones among them perceived that it was disgraceful for grown men, in the midst of a high civilization, to keep up the customs of their barbarian ancestors, who depended on the chase for the means of life. And one ex-earl declared that he had reached the conclusion that a man was dishonored by murdering any creature with less intelligence than himself, unless compelled to do so by absolute hunger.

And so poor, starving, swarming humanity was let loose upon the rabbit-warrens, the deer-parks, and the pheasant-preserves; and houses and gardens arose, as by the touch of an enchanter, where the wilderness had reigned unbroken for thousands of years; and prattling children, rosy and well-fed, took the places of the wild creatures which were God's temporary expedients in an undeveloped world. And the land bubbled over with laughter and sang with happiness. And there was no pale-faced, hungry man or woman in all England. And under the influence of the government all the mills and factories and mines were conducted on coöperative principles, and the word "wages" ceased to be heard in the land and "strikes" were a thing of the barbaric past. And as the paper money poured forth, all forms of enterprise sprang up with marvellous vigor. And the drinking-houses went into bankruptcy, for the intelligent people began to perceive that rum was rottenness, and drunkenness decay and death; and that there was no pleasure that could be wisely bought at the price of impaired intellects, ruined constitutions, and shortened lives. And even the fools perceived that intemperance was simply the counter-impress of the die of misgovernment—the obverse of the medal of bad laws and evil conditions.

And most wonderful of all was the access of thought, the development of literature, the spread of learning, the lifting up of the mind of the great complex races of the British Islands, compounded of many elements, with the inherited culture-capacity drawn from thousands of generations of high civilization in the ancient Atlantean empire. All the past was ransacked for facts and ideas, and the great men of former generations were worshipped with discriminating fervor. And the poorhouses were turned into schools and libraries; for pauperism ended with its parent misgovernment. And the newspapers, instead of being the instrument of an oligarchy, to suppress truth and befog mankind, became the most earnest, zealous advocates of everything that would make men better, happier, and wiser; and in these respects their power was unlimited.

Oh, it was astounding to see how rapidly the human race rose to splendid altitudes of development, as soon as the chains were severed that bound it to the mire. And no man in all the world was any the worse off, eventually, for all this splendid reformation.

CHAPTER XXXV.

SOPHIE'S WORK.

But what was my dear wife doing all this time? Was she idle? Not a bit of it.

In Ireland she insisted upon women's suffrage, and in England, Scotland, and Wales she persuaded them to follow Ireland's example, and make suffrage universal. She argued with great force that the right to vote was not a vanity, or an ornament, or a privilege; but that it meant simply the right of each individual, governed by the laws, to take part in the making of the laws. The Turk, she said, denied women souls, and the Christians had denied them intellect. There was no more reason why women should be excluded from the ballot-box, than there was why she should be denied access to the church or the schoolhouse. She was not only a human being, but the creator of human beings; and to degrade her was to degrade her progeny—mankind. You could not make a great race out of women who thought of nothing but bonnets. There were as many fool-men in the world as there were fool-women, and the one class would never fail to find mates among the other, and thus the charming breed of idiots would be perpetuated to the end of time. You must lift up women if you lift up men.

Sophie also established, in England, Ireland, Scotland, and Wales, a society in every parish for the elevation of women, and she induced the government to set aside annual premiums, of considerable amounts, to the most intelligent women: to the best cooks; to the cleanest housekeepers; to the best mothers; to the best butter-makers, etc. Then she offered similar premiums to the best scholars among the young men; the writers of the best essays, stories, and poems; to the best gardeners, the best farmers, the best mechanics. The whole population was filled with emulation, and such working, writing, scrubbing, gardening, farming never was seen before in the land.

In all these nations she secured an enlargement of the public school system, whereby the best scholars in the parish schools were sent up to the shire highschools, and there supported by the shire-government, while they pursued their studies; and again the selected scholars from the high schools were sent up to and maintained, at the public expense, at the national universities. Out of the highest scholars from these various schools the public offices were filled, under a life tenure, and so, as in China, the poorest child had a chance to rise, without family or political influence, to the highest dignities in the civil service of the state. If youths of either sex displayed special power or ability in any domain of human thought, they were at once made the protégés of the state; and every facility was given them to work out the greatness which God had bestowed upon them. It was a maxim of the government that the nation had no higher function than to develop the genius born among the people—the rarest and most precious gift of God to man.

I need not add that my good wife also transferred to the British Islands her great society to secure to women the fruits of their own industry without the intervention of middlemen. She could not at once close up the awful sores of Whitechapel and the Strand, but by rendering virtue prosperous and happy, she cut off the recruits to the habitations of sin and death. When good and evil are equally profitable there are few women who will not seek out the flowery and peaceful paths of dignity and virtue, rather than the hot and rotten roads which lead down to the hell of personal abasement and disfigurement.

And the people of these islands came to love and revere Sophie as much as did the inhabitants of her native land.

And Sophie also organized a great corps of women to follow the armies, and nurse the wounded and the sick, although, thank God, we had as yet little need for their services.

CHAPTER XXXVI.

THE WRATH OF THE KINGS.

The antiquarians have found, in several instances, the bones of the great extinct monsters of the ancient world stalled in bogs, and surrounded by the remains of fires and the weapons of the hunters who pursued them to the death.

One can fancy the impotent, diabolical wrath of the mastodon or the flying dragon—the giant pterodactyl—the last of their species, as they found themselves encompassed by their puny but powerful enemies, and doomed, helplessly, to certain death. How they must have roared; how their eyes must have flashed, as the darts and arrows struck them; what desperate lunges they must have made, in the treacherous mud, to reach their active foes; how they screamed their last terrific protest against extinction with their last breath.

And so that breed of monsters called kings felt when they read that Ireland, England, Scotland, and Wales had cast down monarchy, aristocracy, and all their trappings, and wrapped their limbs in the pure, white garments of republicanism. Every step of my peaceful advance over the British Islands had been a triumphal march over their sore hearts. They raged and roared while the people exulted. For whom could they trust? The age around them was like a bog in which their cannon sank to the muzzles. Who could set geographical boundaries to the instincts of the human heart? They looked into the faces of the people they and theirs had oppressed for generations, and they could see only lowering brows, distrust, hostility. The very dead seemed, to their excited imaginations, to rise in countless legions, armies, populations, nations, from their crowded graves; and, with chapless jaws, rebuked them for their wasted lives, their starved bodies, their impoverished souls, held in wretched subjugation by them and their cruel ancestors for innumerable generations; and a sweeping wail filled all the universe, and rose to the throne of God, over the lost opportunities and the wrecked lives. It was the resurrection of the sorrows of mankind, the dreadful impeachment of the oppressors of the world.

But the monsters would not yield.

Germany and Austria gathered their forces to stay the advance of the starry flag.

With seven hundred thousand men we landed upon the coast of Belgium and advanced eastward, leaving the friendly republic of France on our right. We passed over the field of Waterloo, where an insular aristocracy grappled with a continental ambition. It was a world-shaking conflict over ignoble objects; a battle not to define the rights of peoples, but the status of dynasties. Napoleon fell and pauperism lived; and thousands have died of misgovernment and wretchedness every year in Europe since, for every man whose life was thrown away on the bloody field of Waterloo. Oh, sacrifice of men to the monsters! The Aztec victims, in their wicker baskets, screaming amid the flames, offered up to Huitzilopochtli—the hideous god of war—are types of humanity in all these latter ages.

We advanced rapidly so as to strike the German army before the forces of Austria could unite with it. From Berlin the young emperor, William, advanced with his splendid legions full of visions of military glory.

CHAPTER XXXVII.

THE BATTLE OF MARBURG.

THE armies encountered each other in the vicinity of Marburg, a town of about 10,000 inhabitants, in the rough and hilly country of Hesse Cassel.

I sent the following letter to the Emperor under a flag of truce:

YOUR MAJESTY :—Without a blow being struck against you or your empire, you united with the aristocracy of England and of other nations to crush the United States of America, and reduce its people to serfdom. You have heard of the fate that has already overtaken the English aristocracy; they fell without a blow. You are forcing your people to fight to maintain the crushing subjugation in which you hold them.

I would avoid the loss of human lives, and I therefore propose that the American army will withdraw from your territory, on condition that, within thirty days from this date, the question of establishing a republican form of government be submitted to a full and free vote of all the people of your empire. If this proposition is accepted, I will appoint a commission to present the question fairly to your people, and to see that it is freely discussed and voted upon, by secret ballot, without intimidation or coercion of any kind. If the majority of your people decide, after such debate, that they prefer the domination of your dynasty to a republican form of government, peace shall be established between the two nations, and our forces will withdraw. An armistice to be declared while such vote is being taken.

I appeal to you, as one who claims to be the affectionate

father of his people, to submit to this peaceful arbitrament. All constitutional power is derived from the people. Let the people say what form of government they prefer.

If you refuse this offer, let the crime of the bloodshed and murder that must follow fall on your head.

I have the honor to be, very respectfully yours,

EPHRAIM BENEZET,
President of the United States of America, and Commander-in-Chief of the Army of Liberation.

So violent was the contempt of the young emperor for all popular rights, that his reply to this peaceful proposition was to fall at once, with tremendous force, upon the left wing of our army. We were taken by surprise. I had supposed, of course, that there would be some negotiation, some respectful reply to my letter.

The first shock of the trained German troops was terrific, and our line was curled back upon itself, and the slaughter was immense. It looked for a while as if a panic had seized our troops.

I was standing upon an elevation, not far from the line of action, and saw the whole scene. The enemy were approaching very close to my own position.

Just at this moment a terrific shout and uproar burst through the tumult from behind me. I turned round and there, a mile away, through a vast cloud of dust, came serried ranks, firing as they advanced.

The enemy had outflanked us, and were attacking us from the rear!

I gave orders at once for the right wing of our army to close in to the aid of the left, and they came on at double-quick.

"Look!" cried one of my aides-de-camp, pointing to the rear.

A surprising thing had happened: the long line of the enemy, which a few minutes before had been advancing upon our rear and firing, had turned their backs and were engaged with troops that were attacking them from behind; they were between two fires, for some of our cannon had been gotten into place and were mowing them down.

And as I looked, lo! the enemy in our rear divided, panic-stricken, and rushed pell-mell to right and left, and through the gap came our triumphant reserves, charging with bayonets lowered, and at their head rode a woman. I looked through my field-glass.

Great God! It was Sophie!

Yes; she had perceived the extremity of our danger, and, forgetting her ambulance corps, had put herself at the head of our reserves, and gave the word—Forward! And they came on like a thunder-storm, sweeping everything before them.

Her face was black with dust, and a bloody handkerchief tied around her left arm showed that she was wounded. But she rode her horse like an amazon, waving her sword, and screaming at the top of her shrill voice—Forward! forward!

She had the genius of command, and instantly gave orders to surround and make prisoners the force of the enemy which was entrapped between our main body and the reserves. Not one of them escaped.

At the same moment I gave orders for a general

advance all along the line, and our vast force rolled forward like a mighty tidal wave. The heroic Germans stood their ground nobly, but nothing could stop the now thoroughly aroused men of the New World, and black and white (for we had whole brigades of negroes under their own officers), with terrible shouts and blazing guns they went forward, and drove back the Germans for two or three miles.

Sophie had saved the army! And I said so in general orders. And the whole army worshipped her. After the fight was over, woman-like, she fainted, and the surgeons had an opportunity to dress her wound, which fortunately was not serious.

As she recovered from her swoon, I stood over her holding her right hand. The fire had all gone out of her eyes, and she looked at me lovingly.

"You are a hero, Sophie!" I said.

"I have one favor to ask," she replied; "give me a division to command. The ecstasy I felt as we broke through that line was worth half a dozen lifetimes."

"You shall have it," I answered.

And it was done. And in her bright uniform she was a picture to look at. And the men! There wasn't one of them that wouldn't have died for her.

"General Sophie!" Lord! how the cry would ring along the lines. I can hear it yet—even in my miseries.

CHAPTER XXXVIII.

THE SECOND DAY OF THE BATTLE.

The emperor was pretty badly crippled. Between killed, wounded, and prisoners he had lost nearly one-third of his army. And the moral loss was even greater than the physical. Besides he had been wounded himself, and had to suffer the loss of his left foot. He lay on a bed of pain, groaning between his set teeth, but as fierce and indomitable as ever;— the heroic representative of an evil system, which was about to pass away from the earth forever.

There were nearly 30,000 prisoners, many of them wounded. We fed them and looked after their injuries with the utmost kindness; they were as well treated as our own men.

We had a printing-press in the camp, run by a small, portable steam-engine.

I wrote and had translated into German the following address, and all night long the press was busy printing them in great quantities. Several were given to each of the prisoners.

Germans:—America loves you. In our ranks are tens of thousands of your countrymen, soldiers of Freedom. In our fair land millions of your people dwell in happy, prosperous homes, in town and country, in woods and prairies, in valleys and on mountain-sides; homes of beauty and delight, where fond hearts bless America and love Germany. Our whole people revere the memories of Goethe and Schiller and Humboldt, and all the other great men of your race who have adorned every department of human thought. We are proud of possessing kindred blood, and tracing back our institutions to the great assemblies of the ancient Germans, as described by Cæsar and Tacitus.

We do not come to oppress or subjugate you. We come to give to all your people the blessings enjoyed by the inhabitants of the United States—education, liberty, fraternity, prosperity

Why should you die that your families may continue slaves to the Hohenzollerns? What is this race of despots to you, that the life-blood of your industry should be forever sucked out of you to maintain them? Why should you pay the cost of a vast standing army, whose principal object is to keep you in subjection, while the work of robbery goes on? How much of the fruits of your own industry have you enjoyed yourselves? How much of it has gone to those who gave you nothing for it? Think upon those questions and answer them in your own hearts

What say you? Will you be free men or slaves? We grieve over every drop of your blood that is shed. We offered your emperor to withdraw if he would submit the question of establishing a republic to the vote of all your people. He replied by attacking us. If this man desires to insist on the subjugation of mankind let him fight it out alone. Or let those aid him who profit by his misgovernment. Let the emperor, the plutocracy, the aristocracy, come out and die for their advantages. Why should you die for them, who are yourselves the very spoil of the great game of oppression?

If we conquer your emperor we will give to every man in Germany a home, a farm, a house, a garden. See what has been done in England, Ireland, and Scotland. If he conquers us, you remain a helpless peasantry.

Do you want a republic? If so, refuse to shoot your liberators. Raise the white flag and march over to the side of the American people. We will receive you like brethren and treat you like men.

EPHRAIM BENEZET,
President of the United States of America, and Commander-in-Chief of the Army of Liberation.

The next morning the prisoners, after giving their parole of honor not to fight against us until exchanged, were provided with a good breakfast and marched back to their own lines, under a flag of truce. Then I sent up half-a-dozen balloons, used for making observations; and, taking advantage of the wind which blew toward the enemy's lines, a white shower of the addresses was let loose and fell all over the German camp. The officers in the balloons reported that they could see, with their glasses, the soldiers running and picking up the papers in all directions, and walking off reading them.

There were a few skirmishes that day, but no pitched battle. My purpose was to give time for the German soldiers to think over what was said in the address, and so I avoided a general action. Spies informed me that night that the emperor was wounded, and that the army was in a demoralized condition, and that, in one instance, an officer had been killed for striking a soldier for insubordination. The men were in a wonderful ferment.

CHAPTER XXXIX.

THE THIRD DAY OF THE CONFLICT.

I FELT certain that the German emperor would order an early attack to stop the spread of the demoralization. The soldiers were drawn principally from the peasantry, and it was well known there had been, for years past, great discontent among them over existing conditions, and at heart they were nearly all republicans. The German inherits from his ancestors a strong love of liberty.

So I was not surprised when, on the morning of the third day, the German army advanced in splendid order against us. An artillery duel, at long range, was followed by the brisk rattle of rifles as the two forces drew nearer together.

Suddenly our men cried out, "They are shooting over our heads!"

And our officers shouted in return, "Fire high!"

It was indeed an extraordinary sight: two armies steadily advancing on each other, amid the blaze of guns, and not a man falling on either side.

I could see the German officers striking the men with their swords and beating down the guns to the proper level, and now and then an officer, unpopular from his arrogance and cruelty, would reel and fall from his saddle, shot by his own men.

And still the battling armies drew nearer and nearer, and great shouts went up from both sides; the Germans crying "America! America!" and our people cheering for Germany. In a moment the two lines met and fraternized, and were in each others' arms, and then such a scene followed as was never witnessed before on a battle-field since time began. All order was lost; the American and German flags were waved together; the men literally swarmed around the joined standards and cheered, and broke into songs; one instant "Der Wacht am Rhein" would ring out in polyglot words from hundreds of thousands of throats, and in a little while "Columbia, the Gem of the Ocean," would be shouted, as if the whole multitude would split their throats.

And far in the background sped away the wounded emperor, surrounded by a few faithful officers of the upper class; a king without a country.

For, as we advanced, the whole people rose up to meet us with cheers and songs. We marched commingled, a regiment of Germans and a regiment of our own men, and a great cry accompanied us, like a wave, ringing from the populace, "Germany is free! Germany is free!"

And it was magnificent to see Sophie riding up and down the line on her white charger. Lord! how they cheered! For every man in his heart worships woman, even as he worships God. For is not woman the representative of God; the life-bringer, the perpetuator, the heart-principle, the lesser creator? God be praised for woman, forever and forever!

Long before we reached Berlin its gates were thrown open to us, for the lightning had told the whole story. The capital welcomed the people; liberty had taken possession of the beautiful city.

CHAPTER XL.

THE DAY OF JUBILEE.

Events followed each other with marvellous rapidity.

The German emperor fled to Austria. On the way he met the Austrian emperor flying from his people. Together they turned their course and made their way to Russia.

Hungary had risen and declared her independence, and was calling for the patriot, Kossuth, despite his great age, to assume the position of president of the new republic. And before the Austrian emperor could rally his forces to suppress the Hungarian revolt, Austria itself had risen in universal rebellion, and the royal family had to fly. Improvised American flags appeared everywhere, and the people shouted like madmen, "America! America!" Wherever the stars and stripes appeared, men and women screamed their applause, their faces wet with tears. The flag meant liberty, justice, fair-play, equal opportunities, prosperity, plenty. All men forgot their toils and troubles; it was an universal holiday—the birth of a new world.

Poland, gallant, persecuted, heroic, noble Poland,

was up in arms from end to end; a Diet had been called to form a constitution, and every man was drilling to meet the hated foe.

And the Irish provisional government telegraphed from Tara to the Polish provisional government at Warsaw:

"Glory be to God in the highest, and on earth peace, good will toward men."

And the government at Warsaw telegraphed to Tara:

"The Spirit of the Lord God is upon me; he hath sent me to preach good tidings into the meek; he hath sent me to bind up the broken-hearted; to proclaim liberty to the captives, and the opening of the prison to them that are bound."

And the king of Denmark telegraphed me to know if he could not keep his throne by making the country otherwise a republic.

And Sophie found the message on my table and answered it with one word:

"SCAT!"

And all Europe roared with laughter, that a Kansas work-girl could cry "Scat!" to a king.

Verily the day of Jubilee had come.

And when the Danish king got Sophie's message, he packed his carpet-bag and lit out for Russia. And the next train held the royal family of Sweden and Norway.

And then I sent a large force, under the command of General Davis of Texas, to Italy; but the Italian monarchy dissolved before our troops reached the boundary of the country. The people had been taxed until they were starved, and it was a physical impossibility to carry on the government farther.

And then came the news of a tremendous uprising in Spain, under the great orator and statesman, Emilio Castelar, and the proclamation of the Spanish republic followed.

And thereupon I issued this decree:

> In the name of the Most High God, and the American people, I, Ephraim Benezet, President of the United States, and Commander-in-Chief of the Army of Liberation, do hereby decree:
> I. The establishment of a new nation, to be called "The United Republics of Europe."
> II. Each republic shall elect two delegates for every million of its population, to meet at Luzerne, Switzerland, on the 15th day of November next, as a constitutional convention, to agree upon the terms of confederation.
> "And they shall beat their swords into ploughshares, and their spears into pruning-hooks; nation shall not lift up sword against nation; neither shall they learn war any more."
>
> EPHRAIM BENEZET.

And a great cry of joy went up from all the people, and men, strangers, embraced each other on the public streets from sheer happiness; for truly it seemed to them that the Day of Jubilee had come, and that the Lord God walked abroad in all the land.

But there was much to be done yet.

And so I constituted a provisional government of "The United Republics of Europe," and noble little

Switzerland, mother of republics, gave us ten miles square upon the shores of Lake Lucerne; and I laid out a great city there, which was called "Liberty" (holding the lots at a nominal price for actual occupants only), and we built a great hall for the coming convention, and the city grew like magic.

And there were millions of men who had been soldiers in the standing armies of the different nations, and who were turned out to starve, and all these I enrolled, temporarily, in the great Army of Liberation, for I saw that all the flying enemies of mankind, emperors, kings, princes and aristocrats, were concentrating in Russia—that land so utterly given over to ignorance, superstition, fanaticism, and despotism that it was to be the last abiding-place of the devil of injustice on earth. And I foresaw that one more great battle, the greatest ever fought in the history of the world, was yet to be waged in Russia, and that there was no argument that would reach the people of that country but the dread, final argument of Force. Napoleon had prophesied, at Saint Helena, that Europe was to become eventually all Tartar or all Republican. The hour of destiny was about to strike on the clock of time. Either we must wipe out that colossal wrong or we must fall before it.

Nothing was won until everything was won. It is true the educated class in that country were Nihilists, for only dynamite could blast a hole in the old walls of that vast despotism, through which the light of liberty might break; but the scholars and thinkers were overwhelmed under the numbers of an ignorant populace, ruled by the most desperate religious bigotry and superstition the world had ever known.

For all the works necessary to be done, and for the support of our vast army, I caused legal-tender paper money of the provisional government of "The United Republics of Europe" to be issued. I could, of course, have created gold coin sufficient for all our wants, but I had already issued such vast quantities of that metal that I feared a depreciation of it in value. Moreover, I desired to familiarize the world with the use of national "greenbacks," and pave the way for that day when metallic money would cease to exist. I believed that it was the duty of government to supply the people with a medium of exchange that would rest purely on the *fiat* of the government; the same *fiat* that could take all the possessions of the citizen and shove him forward to the front of battle to be slain; the same *fiat* which, through its courts, settled all questions of property and right between citizens, and sent the guilty to the scaffold or the guillotine; that *fiat* which was the greatest earthly power known in the affairs of man.

After some millions of paper money of the provisional government had been put forth, the bankers of Europe—whom I had left undisturbed in the pursuit of their business—entered into a conspiracy to stop the progress of events by refusing to take it, on the ground that no fund of gold had been provided for its redemption; and they laughed and chuckled among themselves immensely, when they thought that they had brought battle-fields and universal public opinion to naught, by their little shop-trick.

I immediately telegraphed to every city in Europe to seize upon all the money in the vaults of all the banks, and close up those institutions, and I issued the following decree:

Whereas, a lot of bankers, who have not the courage to resist the advance of mankind in open war, have attempted to arrest it, by discrediting the paper money issued by a power great enough to take their worthless lives;

And whereas, they have done this on the pretence that no fund in gold has been provided for the redemption of said paper money:

And whereas, the government is desirous to satisfy the honest scruples of all men;

It is therefore decreed.

I. That all banking houses of issue or deposit are hereby forever abolished in Europe, and no person shall deal in moneys except the duly appointed agents and officers of the government.

II. Every existing banking corporation is hereby placed in the hands of a receiver, to be appointed by the provisional government, whose duty it shall be to first repay to the citizens all deposits made with such banking house, and collect all debts due them; and all the property, moneys, and effects of said banking houses and the corporators or members thereof, are hereby confiscated, to be used as a guarantee fund for the paper money of the provisional government, so that hereafter no man shall say that it is not perfectly safe and worth the face of the same.

III. In addition to the postal savings banks now in use in most of the nations, there is hereby established, in every town of over 5,000 inhabitants, a sub-treasury, to receive deposits, make loans, and buy and sell exchange; it being the object of the government to prevent, as far as possible, the government's instrumentalities of exchange, for the facilitation of commerce, being seized upon, monopolized, and turned into a commodity, so that they cannot be used by the public without paying tribute to individuals.

EPHRAIM BENEZET,

President of the United States, and President of the Provisional Government of the United Republics of Europe.

How all the nations laughed over the way in which I satisfied the scruples of the bankers! And how the bankers roared with grief and terror, when they realized how impotent their tricks were in the iron grasp of power! And what a vast fund of billions of dollars rolled into the national treasury, and was lent out at two per cent per annum to encourage business enterprises of all kinds! And how prosperity leaped forward, released from those bloodsucking vampires, the usurers!

And everywhere the land was subdivided, and railroads built to open up new territories to settlement, and houses and gardens were created as if by magic, and the whole land laughed with happiness.

And the national debts! There was, indeed, a problem. Misgovernment; villanous, unnecessary wars; corruption; the mistresses and bastards of kings; the vices and rottenness of courts, had heaped them up until it became a physical impossibility for the people to pay the interest upon them. The whole productive power of the continent was unequal to the task. Nature had repudiated them before the national governments could act upon them. They fell of their own weight.

Upon my recommendation each nation appointed a commission, which took testimony to show where the failure to pay the interest on the national debt would work destitution and actual want to individuals who had all their fortunes invested in such funds; and in these cases a reasonable pension was paid during the life-time of the sufferers. But otherwise the governments had no interest in the preservation of colossal fortunes, which gave men power for evil over their fellows. What was needed was not a few greatly rich, but all greatly happy. A millionaire represents the farthest swing of the pendulum from a pauper; one was the cause and the correlative of the other. What was needed was to abolish both. And we did it.

And the anarchists disappeared. They represented simply the protest of passionate men against horrible conditions. They were like those who, to escape the crushing miseries of life, kill themselves. They were ready to blow up a dreadfully misgoverned world with dynamite.

And the whole land swarmed with men, learned and unlearned, who propounded a thousand plans for the betterment of man's condition. But the press and the ballot-box were open to them all, and all Europe became a great debating school, where one after the other they exposed each other's impracticable schemes, and eliminated out of the uproar and confusion those things which stood the test of discussion and were good for humanity. And a mighty spirit of philanthropy swept over the whole land; and man was no longer a drug; a creature to be squeezed down by "the iron law of wages" into a pauper's grave; a something to be booted and kicked and starved off the face of the planet. And the beauty and grandeur of humanity, "so infinite in faculty, in form and motion, so express and admirable; in action so like an angel; in apprehension so like a god, the beauty of the world, the paragon of animals," became patent to all men, even to those who held their noses highest in the world. And the peasant's child, with its bright eyes and rounded limbs and glowing hair, was a fairer sight than the sculptured gods of the ancient Athenians. For Divinity shone in every line of the renewed, rejuvenated, and redeemed humanity.

CHAPTER XLI.

ARMAGEDDON.

But all this time I was gathering up my faculties for the last great conflict.

Nine toes of the image of Daniel—England, Spain, Germany, Austria, Portugal, Sweden, and Norway, Denmark, Greece, and Italy, had crumbled; the iron and clay had been dissolved, and only one more, Russia, the biggest toe of all, remained. But I knew that God had foreordained, thousands of years ago, that "the stone cut out of the mountain without hands" should fall upon and crush it. And is not our republic, resting upon the broad base of the popular will, a mountain, culminating in the sharp crest of concentrated authority? And had not the American republic been built without hands, save only the hands of the Almighty? It was not made. It grew inevitably out of its surroundings. No man can put his finger down and say, "Here liberty and constitutional government began." Its principles were born before the colonists left their ships.

I gathered two million men in Poland. I believed with Napoleon that the best way to conduct a defensive warfare was by offensive measures. I proposed to attack the Russian bear in his den.

Our forces stretched from Grodno to Wilna. We seized upon the great railway running from Warsaw to St. Petersburg. The troops of the Czar gathered to the defence of their capital. They tore up the tracks and burned the bridges as we advanced. But what was that to Yankees? Our ranks contained men of every pursuit known to civilization, and every workman was intelligent enough to command. The fruits of the public-school system, continued through serveral generations, had added one hundred percentage to the powers of the race. As the track was torn up, we relaid it; as the bridges were burned we rebuilt them. We had the granaries and forests of Poland to draw upon. The poorest peasant offered all he had freely. This was the world's battle, and every man understood it.

What an army it was! In the centre were the victors of Canada and Germany, white and black, under the command of General Taubeneck of Illinois. The right wing was made up of Frenchmen, Germans, and Italians, under General Washburn of Massachusetts; the left wing, under General Gaither of Alabama, was composed of Scandinavians, Austrians, Spaniards, Portuguese, and even Moors from beyond the Mediterranean. The reserves were under the command of Sophie; they were made up of choice troops from all parts of Europe.

It was impossible to move so vast a host in any

small area, and while we used the great railway to carry forward supplies, our extreme right reached nearly to Minsk, and our skirmishers on the left touched upon Kovna. The peasants fled as we advanced into the Russian provinces, and the few captured by our troops were sullen and hostile. Some of our straggling soldiers, when we reached the province of Pskov, were killed, beaten to death by the brutalized inhabitants. The country was flat and sandy, with many swamps, which divided our forces more than was desirable.

At Ostrov we met the advance guard of the Russian army. Some skirmishing followed, and I began to concentrate our forces.

It was time, for at daybreak the Russian army fell upon our centre with terrible force and impetuosity, led by the Czar in person. Soon our entire line was engaged, and as fresh troops came up they were moved into place. It was a terrible conflict. We soon found we had no children to deal with. The Russian soldiers fought with fanatical, dogged fury, and died with the spirit of martyrs. It was terrible to see such enthusiasm wasted in behalf of ignorance and despotism. The god-like in man can be perverted into the devil-like.

All day long the battle raged and the slaughter on both sides was fearful. Night put an end to the conflict, and we found time to bury our dead.

There was led into my tent about midnight a Russian officer who had surrendered himself to our picket guard. He was a handsome man, with a most determined countenance. His name was Alexis Karsinoff; he was a major in the troops from Nishni-Novgorod. He told me, in French, that he was a Nihilist, and that the greater part of the officers of his part of the army were Nihilists.

They had agreed that the only way to defeat the Russian army, and secure liberty for their afflicted country, was to kill the Czar in the heat of battle. This would demoralize the fanatical peasants. They had selected one of their number, a colonel in the royal body-guard (he did not give his name), to slay the Czar in the midst of the next day's fight. And he had come to tell me, so that the moment the panic appeared, which was certain to follow the act, I might press the advantage and win the victory.

I shuddered as the major coolly told me his story.

"The American army cannot profit by assassination," I said.

"Nor would we," he replied, "if we were free. But what can we do? One man sits on the neck of millions. We are denied the ballot-box, free press, free speech, the right of assembly, even the right to humbly petition for the improvement of our condition or the redress of grievances; while the Greek church is the shameless ally of this despotism, and keeps the wretched peasantry in ignorance and superstition, that they may be the more readily controlled by the government. It is a conspiracy of bigotry and force against mankind. We have no remedy but assassination. It is that or submission. The crime be upon the heads of those who have denied us any other way of protesting against injustice. Is it not better that a few should die if thereby millions may be made happy for all time?"

"Unhappy men," I replied, "I perceive the difficulties of your position. No man has a right to life at the cost of the moral and physical death of all his countrymen. But the American army cannot win victories by the aid of murder. I shall feel it my duty to warn the Czar of his impending danger. At the same time you are free to go or stay at your pleasure."

He asked permission to remain and fight as a private in our ranks. This was granted him, and he withdrew.

At daybreak a flag of truce bore the following letter to the Russian lines:

To THE CZAR:—I would be glad to see you dead, for you stand in the way, blocking the advance of civilization. You live at the cost of uncountable suffering to your fellow-men. But there is a wide difference between war and assassination. I therefore notify you that information has come to me that your officers are honeycombed with Nihilism, and that one of your body-guard has been selected to kill you to-day in the heat of battle. Be on your guard.
EPHRAIM BENEZET,
President of the United States.

The Czar, as I learned afterward, read this letter, scowled on those around him, and placed it in his bosom. It was found there after his death.

The sun had not yet risen when the battle was resumed with terrible fury. All morning it raged with varying fortunes. We hurled army after army upon that huge, stolid, living wall, but in vain. The dead were piled in ramparts between the combatants.

It was plain to be seen that we outnumbered the enemy, but their courage was magnificent.

I sent an order to Sophie:

Send 50,000 infantry, with artillery and cavalry, to move around the right flank of the enemy and fall upon them in the rear.
EPHRAIM BENEZET.

A French subaltern, dusty and haggard, rode up to me and handed me this note, written on the inside of an old envelope:

I am coming, one hundred thousand strong. Charge to meet me.
SOPHIE.

I was near one of the points of observation, from which anchored balloons had been sent to a great height, communicating with the earth by fine telegraph wires.

I telephoned the officer in the balloon to watch the rear of the right flank of the enemy, and keep me informed of what he saw.

It was one hour before I received any message from the balloon. Then it came:

MR. PRESIDENT:—There is now—1:30 P.M.—a great dust cloud rising all along the horizon, in the rear of the Russian army. It seems to be caused by large masses of armed men, probably reinforcements of the enemy.

J. A. FONTLEROY,
Col. Commanding Balloon 271.

I had scarcely read it before another aide dashed up from the field telegraph station, and handed me a slip of paper. It read:

MR. PRESIDENT:—At this time—1:45 P.M.—the dust cloud resolves itself into hundreds of thousands of armed men.

1:55 o'clock P.M.—Hurrah! Our glasses show they carry the American flag. They are coming on the run. It is an immense host.

J. A. FONTLEROY,
Col. Com. Balloon 271.

Another furious rider dashed up with a message in his hand:

2 o'clock P.M.

MR. PRESIDENT:—They are within one mile of the Russian rear. The cannon have opened on the foe. A woman rides at their head, on a white horse. Hurrah! It is General Sophie!

J. A. FONTLEROY.

"God bless her!" I shouted.

Right and left the aides flew, and soon the field telegraph lines carried the orders for a general advance.

"Forward, forward, boys! forward," I cried, as I sprang to my horse.

The telegraph had done its work. A wave of ringing cheers rose above the thunder of our cannon, responded to by faintly heard cheers, and the booming of artillery beyond the Russian lines. What a sight it was as our many-colored tidal-wave of men rolled forward upon the devoted Russians!

I spurred to the front on our left flank, intending to unite with the forces led by Sophie, and in a few moments I was in the thick of the dreadful carnage. The weight of our numbers and the impetus of our charge carried us crashing through the Muscovite lines; but they were heroes, those barbarians, and they stood back to back, defending themselves from the attacks from front and rear.

And then I caught sight of Sophie!

She was rushing forward among the broken ranks of the Russ. It was a magnificent sight. Her white horse spurned the earth; her eyes flashed with the fire of battle; her dark hair flew on the wind behind her; her sword waved in the air.

My God! She is down!

A Russian cannon-ball struck the white steed full in the breast and tore it assunder.

She is killed!

No; I can see her on one knee, struggling to disengage her foot from the stirrup. The soldiers swarm around to protect her with their bodies.

Then I saw a gigantic Polander, from Kovno, seize her in his huge arms, as if she were a child, and place her upon his shoulders.

She was unhurt! I could hear the roar of applause and laughter where I stood. She buried her left hand in the mop of yellow hair of the giant to steady herself, waved her sword, and in her high, ringing voice shouted, "Forward!"

The wave of men had paused when she fell, and a great "Oh!" rose from a hundred thousand brawny breasts, as if each man had been himself struck; but Lord! how they sprang forward with the towering giant at their head, and Sophie on his shoulders, her sword glittering like a meteor over death and glory.

"Forward! forward!" rang the cry.

And the Muscovites! They did not fly; they did not yield. No; they stood in their tracks and were hewn down for God and the Church. Their courage was magnificent.

And at that moment the brawny, bearded Colonel Tischinoff, cool as an icicle, and his small black eyes, deep-set, glowing like sparks of fire, rode up to the Czar, close up to him, and drawing a revolver shot him squarely through the head. And before the astonished officers could draw sword, he placed the pistol to his own head and fell a corpse beside the dead emperor!

And then the panic!

"The Czar is dead! The Czar is dead!" rang the cry.

It was as if men had shouted to those beleaguered, fanatical peasants, "God is dead!" For the Czar was their god.

Some ran wildly, unarmed, and threw themselves upon the bayonets of their foes. Others fled to the hill-top, cast away their guns, and surrendered.

All is over.

No; not all. For then came a sight the ages will love to paint forever!

Down over the thickly strewn field, carpeted with the dead and dying, came a great army of men.

Sophie, on her strange steed, rode at the head. Forehead and cheeks and chin were black with war-dust and smoke; but her eyes and the straight array of pearly teeth shone out of the disfigurement. And she laughed aloud in a wild ecstasy, and patted the giant's yellow head, as one might the mane of a favorite steed. And the Polander roared! His open mouth in the midst of his bearded face looked like a cave in the side of a bushy hill. And he rolled his eyes up as to a divinity.

Oh! his posterity for twenty generations will tell the tale of this day's work.

And the multitude!—the vast array laughed and in a dozen dialects shouted "The Queen! The Queen!"

And Sophie saw me. And, leaning forward, she took the giant by his great, bulbous nose and steered him straight to me.

And when she came where I stood, surrounded by acres of hurrahing and exulting soldiers, she leaped lightly from the Polander's shoulders, and flung herself into my arms, and kissed me before them all, and cried:

"Didn't we give it to 'em! Oh, if Kansas could have seen it!"

"The world saw it, Sophie, and will continue to see it forever."

Yes! A Yankee woman had won Armageddon! A Western girl had achieved the Millennium!

The thousand years of peace and happiness and love had begun, amid the corpses of that bloody battle-field; the last battle-field of the ages.

CHAPTER XLII.

THE MILLENNIUM.

From St. Petersburg I put forth this proclamation:

The people must prepare themselves to enjoy unending peace and liberty.

The greatest danger to the nations is ignorance. Universal education is the basis of all progress.

The highest crime known to mankind is to keep the people in mental darkness.

Let all doctrines be tested by investigation, and that which is true will endure, and that which is false will perish. We cannot maintain error at the sacrifice of mankind. An ignorant mind is a reproach to man, and an offence and a pollution to God.

Great Father! Thou hast given us liberty. Give us light! Let thy fiat go forth as in the old days when thou saidst: "'Let there be light,' and there was light."

Let every brain shine like an electric lamp in the midst of the twilight of nature. Let every soul be a temple of knowledge of thee and thy marvelous and boundless works. Thou hast swept away our rulers; make us fit, by wisdom and learning, to rule ourselves. Let us never forget that when we delegate to another the task of thinking we appoint our master and enthrone our tyrant. He who thinks for us will inevitably, eventually, take the profits of our industry. To be free we must be fit to be free. All else is mockery and deception—"leather and prunella."

Every child in Russia must have education; and he that stands in the way, be he priest or prelate, shall perish. If there is anything in the creeds of men that will not bear the light of day, away with it it is accursed. God's truth cannot undo man's truth. Intelligence is fatal only to superstition.. That which falls before the advance of knowledge is only error. Light! Light! Let the world have universal light!

> "God works in all things; all obey
> His first propulsion from the night.
> Wake thou and watch! The world is gray
> With morning light."

All injustice is from this day abolished in Russia. The land will be divided in small tracts among the actual occupants, and houses will be built for them. But any man who, at the end of ten years, cannot prove that he is able to read and write, will forfeit his possessions, unless he is over seventy years of age at the date of this proclamation. Public free schools shall be established for every two hundred scholars, youths and adults. All things are for the intelligent; nothing for the voluntary ignorant. The people must use their brains or get off the land; the illiterate and the vicious have no right to cumber the earth; they exist upon it only by the toleration of their fellows. Every man must contribute the fruits of his intelligence to the advance of the whole mass.

Ephraim Benezet,

President of the United States and President of the Provisional Government of the United Republics of Europe."

I felt sure that if we could compel the Russian people to read and write, for three years, we would break down the horrible power of the Greek church, which had for centuries held them in ignorance and squalor, the abject and unreasoning slaves of the worst despotism on earth, and the devout followers of childish fables which were enough to make the whole world roar with laughter.

There were in southern and eastern Russia vast regions of country possessing a fertile soil, but uninhabited, because of the distance from railroads and the affliction of droughts. They had been owned by great lords and were not worth a penny an acre. These I confiscated, built long lines of railroad through them, laid out cities on my usual plan; divided the land into small tracts; built houses and settled in them the soldiers who had belonged to the standing armies of the different nations. I foresaw that if these vast masses of men were left unemployed, they would press upon and impoverish labor, breed discontent, and create turbulence. But, believing that race-clannishness was altogether evil, I interspersed the different nations with each other, and compelled the teaching of English in all the schools. Thus in the next generation there would be a mingling of race-stocks, with a consequent vast increase of the powers of the human race, physical and mental; and they would all be able to speak the same language, and that the language destined to become the universal tongue of the world. Dialects are like mountain chains and rivers; they serve to divide and antagonize mankind. They are all of them barbarian variations, born of isolation and ignorance, out of the parent tongue of "Atlantis," the antediluvian world, of which Aryan is one of the earliest forms. Civilization is tunnelling the mountains and bridging the rivers and commingling all men into one great homogeneous whole. Let it wipe out the geographical, dialectical peculiarities, and enable all the inhabitants of the earth to communicate with each other in one tongue. Supplement this with electricity, and the whole planet will be as a brain, its cerebral gray-matter on its surface; a mass that will think, tied together by universal threads of fire; while the globe will be held in the hand of God for the delight of his swarming angels; for thought is as veritable a reality in nature as light or heat—yea, more.

Lord! what a glory it will be, in the fullness of time, for him who can speak to and be heard by such a world! Beside it all things in the past will be petty, provincial, insignificant.

The amount of arable land was greatly increased, for these and similar colonies, by using the discovery by which, in the western American States, rain has been repeatedly produced at will.

The air lies in strata, oftentimes moving in different directions. Very often a stratum or current of air, heavily charged with moisture, passes over an arid region of country, moving over the face of another stratum of very dry air of a different temperature. If now there can be sent up from the earth a column of some light and volatile gas, it penetrates, like a chimney, through the different strata, commingling them one with another, and bringing down the condensed moisture in the form of rain on the thirsty soil.

By this means, government taking charge of the rain-making, we were able to extend our colonies into regions heretofore considered unfit for human habitation. In fact, by this tremendous discovery, it is possible to turn Sahara itself into a garden of beauty, and vastly enlarge man's dominion over the earth. For there is scarcely any part of the earth's surface, except the bare rocks of the mountain chains, and the desolate recesses of the north, that will not sustain human life, if given warmth and moisture enough.

The whole surplus population of Europe was thus soon packed away in great colonies, to their infinite happiness and contentment, and the betterment of the condition of the rest of the population. Universal opportunity and exact justice bred universal peace and prosperity.

CHAPTER XLIII.

CHRISTIANITY.

AND it seemed to me that the new birth of mankind, which I had helped to bring about, needed a new birth of religion.

For what is man if not a creature of the spiritual world, temporarily loaned to the material world by its great Designer. The man who proclaims himself a brother of the beast, and no more, abases himself, not humanity. Who is so blind that he cannot see the tremendous spirit of man shining through the clay? Can clay think, reason, worship? No; not in a million years. That which is within the clay is that which thinks, reasons, worships; it is man; nothing else can be.

And Christianity! How can we frame a reform that shall transcend that august creed: "*Love God with all thy heart and thy neighbor as thyself*"?

"Love God with all thy heart."

The spirit of man clinging, amid the perturbations of the flesh, to the spirit of the universe.

"Love thy neighbor as thyself."

Immortal creed! Words to be written in all human constitutions, as they lie at the base of all human progress. Civilization can never rise above the level of Christianity.

But what is Christianity now? Warring sects and bitter factions, tearing each other to pieces:

> Fragments of one golden world,
> Yet to be re-lighted in its place in heaven.

The spirit of Divinity lost in the glosses of the ages. Christ forgotten in the passions of a disgraceful dog-fight of sects.

Should not the Millennium begin with it a new birth of Christianity? Should not the creeds find some common ground whereon they could work for the good of man and the glory of God? Was it possible to revive the very spirit, thought, and purpose of the Founder, so long obscured and buried by barbarian epochs?

To think was with me to act.

I issued at once this appeal:

To All Christian People on the Planet:—

It seemeth me to be unreasonable and blasphemous, that while there is so much good to do, and so much evil to resist, those who call themselves Christians should be enemies to each other, and hence divided and powerless. Is there no means whereby mutual charity can unite them to do Christ's work on earth, in peace and harmony? Is their hatred of each other greater than their opposition to evil? If so, they are not Christians, but children of the devil, sons of Belial.

Law can prevent crime and insure justice, but it has its limitations. It deals not with thoughts, but acts. It can regulate the opening and shutting of the doors of the temple of the soul, but it cannot enter in and purify the polluted chambers. Only that which connects man with the vast spirit·

ual brotherhood around him can do that mighty work. No reform of legislation is complete which is based on a beast-world, without conscience. Besides a fair division of the rights and goods of the world there must be a something vaster and profounder—man's *love* for his fellow—not merely a willingness to give him a fair show and a fair divide, but an *affection* for him, reaching from heart to heart. Love is the stamp which God sets on his work. Love is nature's testimony to the existence of God; for in itself there is no reason why selfish brutality should love anything. Love is a winged thing, that comes out of and soars above and, with the brightness of its pinions, glorifies the base animal necessities of the clay-wrought creature man.

There can be no permanent governmental reform which is not built upon the grand maxim: "Love God with all thy heart and thy neighbor as thyself." There must be first goodness before there can be greatness. If the people are evil the laws cannot be good. The wickedness of a generation will overcome the justice of the statutes.

With a purpose, therefore, that the heart and brain of man shall advance together, I request that each religious, Christian denomination, of each nation in the world, shall select delegates, in such manner as may seem to it fit and best, equally divided between clerics and laymen, upon the basis of one delegate for every hundred thousand of membership, to meet on Christmas Day next, at the city of Washington, in the United States of America, there to take counsel together for the following purposes:

I. For the promotion of a charitable Christian spirit among all the denominations, overlooking whatever may have been evil in the record of each other, as due to the imperfections of man, and as not being an essential part of the spirit of true religion.

II. To seek out some common basis of belief; agreeing to agree where they can, even though they differ where they must.

III. In this way to reëstablish Christianity as a practical whole, relegating dogmatic differences to the consideration of each separate denomination.

IV. To unite the whole force of all who believe in Christ in an effort to fight evil, repress injustice, dispense charity, increase intelligence, and promote the happiness, prosperity, and goodness of mankind.

V. To establish in every province and parish of the Christian world a brotherhood devoted to these great ends, and who shall also labor to maintain the governmental reforms which have already resulted in such incalculable benefits to the world.

And upon this undertaking I invoke the blessing of Almighty God and the approval of all good men.

EPHRAIM BENEZET.

The idea spread like wildfire. The plan of reuniting all Christians, and placing Christ above creed, and works above dogma, appealed to every breast. The vision of a consolidated Christianity, laboring everywhere for the good of the human race, thrilled a million souls. Many earnest and faithful clergymen had long felt that the churches had fallen behind in the race of reform, and were losing their grip on the hearts of men; they perceived that sin was largely the result of human injustice, selfishness, and the inequalities produced by, or not prevented by law; that poverty bred microbes of the soul as well as of the body; that misgovernment drove more swarming souls into hell than all the weaknesses and vanities of the flesh; and that the wrongs done by man to himself were venial, compared with those which he practised upon his brother.

All over the earth men began to seek out the points upon which the several creeds agreed, and to forget those wherein they differed. And essays and books were written to palliate and excuse the dark passages in each other's history. And a beautiful spirit of charity and toleration spread over the world, associated with a firm adherence, nevertheless, to that which each one thought right. And the word *Christian* had a new and broader significance than it ever possessed before; and there was a sense of brotherhood between all who bore the name, and Christ walked anew in the hearts of the children of men.

And so men prepared themselves for the thousand years of peace and love and justice foretold by the seers and prophets of old.

CHAPTER XLIV.

THE UNIVERSAL REPUBLIC.

But still, in the midst of all these happy surroundings, one thing troubled me.

It was the fear that sooner or later the nations would differ and quarrel, and as there was no tribunal to which all would submit, wars must follow, and once the old sore of the world was opened who could tell when it would close? There were the differences which might arise between countries over boundary lines; and the clash of contending commercial interests, and internal rebellions; and the ambitions of bad and able men; and the natural wickedness and meanness of the human animal, with all its inherited ape-like traits; and there too, above all, was the spirit of evil, which seems to be woven into all the warp and woof of the universe.

How could we make peace certain and perpetual?

That was the question.

At length, after many cogitations, I hit upon this plan.

There were the Azore Islands. They had been the mountain peaks of the drowned "Atlantis," whose history was told by the Greek priests to Solon, and recorded for posterity by Plato; the great world that lies in the background of human history; the mighty empire said to have been drowned by God for its sins.

These islands are beautiful, with a paradisiacal climate; a garden of delights — the Hesperides. Where could the capital of the world be better located than on one of these charming isles, with the drowned empire beneath the waves at its feet, a perpetual reminder of the wickedness of man and the justice of God?

And so I secured from the little republic of Portugal, by purchase, the island of St. Michael, the largest of the group, and situated about eight hundred miles west of the coast of Spain.

And then I issued to every republic in the world, in Europe, Asia, North America, South America, and Australia, a proposal that they should all unite and form "The Universal Republic," whose capital should be on the island of St. Michael.

This should be a government of limited powers, ceded to it by the component republics, for the preservation of the peace of the world.

Under its constitution there should be a President and Cabinet, and a Congress of several hundred members, one for each million of inhabitants, to be elected by the people of the different nations. This Congress should be the ultimate court of appeal in disputes between the confederated republics, and all parties were to pledge themselves to peacefully accept its conclusions.

"The Universal Republic" should protect each nation in its established rights, boundaries, etc.; it should secure to each a republican form of government; it should aid in the suppression of internal rebellions; it should maintain a small army and navy, with power to call upon its constituent powers for further naval or military forces when necessary. It should have the further right to communicate with the congresses of each nation, and offer, from time to time, such advice as it saw fit, upon matters essential to the welfare of the people; but with no power to otherwise interfere in the domestic affairs of a country, except where a nation refused to submit to its decrees, under appeal, in contests with another republic.

The advantages of such a system were to substitute arbitration for war, and to insure unbroken peace for many generations, if not forever. If one country became arrogant and oppressive, the power of the whole confederation could be brought to bear to crush it. The members of the Congress were to hold their seats for ten years, and to be paid large salaries. It was the intention to make these places the highest and noblest in the gift of the people. The President was to be elected by the direct vote of all the people of all the republics, and to hold his office for six years. As disputes between nations would probably occur but seldom, a chief function of the new government would be to observe wherein any nation, from any cause, fell below the true standard of a free people in point of education, virtue, enterprise, industry or otherwise, and by bringing to bear upon it an enlightened public opinion, compel such government to keep pace with the general march of progress. "The Universal Republic" would thus be a monitor and adviser for all, and the poorest people, in the most remote regions, would feel the influence of its beneficent prescience.

It seemed to me that, with such a system, peace, order, and the highest civilization would endure on earth until some cosmical catastrophe wiped the human family off the planet, in another "Ragnarök."

CHAPTER XLV.

WE PREPARE TO GO BACK TO AMERICA.

SOPHIE was delighted when I told her we were about to return to the United States. I said to her that I must present to the great American Republic two schemes. First I must persuade the people to vote to enter "The Universal Republic;" and secondly, I must get them to assent to another proposition, which I had long cherished, to wit, an international agreement, among all the civilized countries, for the establishment of a universal paper money, to be issued in a certain fixed ratio to population by each nation, and to be legal-tender in every nation on earth. I argued that a currency of this kind, circulating everywhere, with all the property of the world pledged to make it good, and the fiat of all the nations behind it, would supersede all forms of metallic money, and would increase in amount with the increase of population; and thus put an end forever to all financial panics and convulsions, and be the greatest boon which statesmanship could confer on the commercial world.

Each nation, under existing conditions, possessed an admirable currency within its own borders, but the moment it reached the boundary line its power was crippled. Hence men clung to a "precious" metal, which, as a commodity, could be exchanged from nation to nation, like wheat or cotton. But if France, Germany, Italy, Brazil, Canada, the United States, and all the rest, agreed to give to English paper money (provided a certain amount *per capita* was not exceeded), the same validity they gave to their own money; and if England agreed to treat the other nations the same way; and if the same system was applied to every republic in the world, then the money-changers could no longer stand at the gateways of the nations and compel all men to bow down and worship their yellow god, and thus chain the industry of the world to his Juggernaut car. And, as I argued, such an international treaty could provide a central commission that would stamp the paper money, as issued, and see that no nation exceeded the quota to which it was entitled.

But all these things I must talk over with our intelligent American people, and meet the objections which ten thousand shrewd minds would advance: for the Yankees—glory be to God!—take nothing for granted, and they are no hero-worshippers. [I use the word "Yankee" in its continental sense.] They must have a reason for everything. And why not:

> Sure, He, who made us with such large discourse,
> Looking before and after, gave us not
> That capability and godlike reason
> To rust in us unused.

The man who will not think when he can doesn't deserve to live.

But before I left Europe I restored Palestine to the Jews; adding the ancient provinces of their old-time kinsmen, the Phœnicians, including the abandoned sites of Tyre and Sidon.

It seemed to me that this great race, the Israelites, from whom we had derived our religion and so much of our literature, should have some share in the awakening of the world. They are a trading, not an agricultural, people; and so I told them to plant themselves in the ancient seats of commerce, at the head of the Mediterranean, between India, China, and Australia on the one hand, and Europe and America on the other, with the Mediterranean Sea for a harbor and the Suez Canal for a gateway, and revive the ancient glories of their people. I gave orders that all Jewish emigrants to the Holy Land should be carried free, with their effects, over the government railroads; that the land should be divided among them; houses built; railroads and ships constructed; a national convention held at Jerusalem, and financial help extended to make them at once a great and prosperous people. And out from all the lands of hatred and persecution the poor afflicted Hebrews, with their wives and little ones, poured in a steady stream into the old lands of their race; wealthy Israelites helped them, and natural leaders sprang up among them; and it will be but a little time until the Jews, too, shall have a nation and a flag, illustrious and honored in the world; while the smoke of their steamers shall ascend from every sea and every harbor on the globe. And their delegates shall hold high seats, too, in the Congress of "The Universal Republic," respected as representatives of the race which preserved the worship of one true God in the midst of the darkness and foulness of ages of barbarism.

CHAPTER XLVI.

WE VISIT ENGLAND AND IRELAND.

Our journey was one continued ovation; whole nations turned out to honor us, especially Sophie, who had won all hearts.

Through Germany and France we passed. The populace unhitched the horses at every town, and drew our carriage; and the streets were one mass of huzzaing, excited people; the air white with waving handkerchiefs.

We crossed over into England and the same scenes followed.

Everywhere the same story was told us of unbounded prosperity. Industry, relieved of its burdens, had bounded forward with a giant's strength. Pauperism had disappeared; joy and plenty shone in every face; the whole land laughed.

London was a sight to see. Never before had it known such growth and prosperity. The vast sullen, chalky-faced hordes of the underfed unemployed, who used to block up the streets, were gone; they were busy in shops and factories, or out in pleasant little homes on thousands of farms, consumers of the productions of their brethren. The mere appreciation in the values of all forms of property, by the decrease in the purchasing-power of money, due to its greater abundance, had made millions prosperous or rich, and had lifted up the very mendicants, by making room for them in the ranks above them. Even the bankers were growing richer by the vast increase in all sorts of industrial enterprises, and by the greater activities of commerce. The ancient bugaboo that man liberated was more dangerous than man enslaved, had been exploded. Even the timorous discovered, to their astonishment, that the most peaceful creature on earth is a human being with his belly full; and that men take to carrying dynamite in their pockets when they can get nothing else to put in them. Absolute justice, it was demonstrated, was society's best constable and soldier. Men revolt against evil, not against favorable conditions.

And the country! What a sight it was! Fields, gardens, houses everywhere; every spadeful of earth cultivated; the land alive with people; hopeful people, joyous people, people thanking God and loving their fellows.

And the new English Parliament was in session; it was only one house, for the people did not believe in placing clogs on their own action. They gave us a grand reception. What a fine array of solid heads and serious faces; mechanics, farmers, business men; every man thoughtful, reasonable, and earnest; a magnificent, self-governing race.

And so we passed over to Dublin. The ancient

city put on its holiday clothes to greet us; the green flag was everywhere, and the impassioned people were ready to jump out of their skins with enthusiasm.

And then, by the new railway, we passed on to Tara, through continuous fields and gardens and swarming people; a beautiful land, greatly blessed of God, but long afflicted by man; every acre fertilized by the blood of its unhappy inhabitants; but now gay as a fair, and forgetting its dreadful past in its new joys and hopes; a light-hearted, generous, magnanimous race; deeply touched by kindness, but meeting oppression with a courage and persistence which a thousand years had not been able to overcome.

The whole land dropped its pursuits and followed us to Tara. And what a city had arisen in a few months on the old earth-heaps! Great numbers of Irishmen had come back from America, bringing wealth with them, to help build up their native land with transatlantic energy.

The whole people seemed to have assembled at Tara to greet us; a vast concourse like that which in the ancient days gathered around the high-king.

The great hall was built after the antique fashion; it was ornamented with the horns of deer, and the prodigous antlers of the extinct gigantic elk. Upon the platform was the harp of Brian Boroimhe, brought from the Royal Irish Academy, and placed under a glass case. On the walls were the portraits of hundreds of men famous in Irish history, from St. Patrick to the present day. On a raised *dais* on one side were harpers and bagpipers, clad in the ancient costumes, and discoursing the quaint music of the past.

The scene as Sophie and I walked up the main hall was one never to be forgotten. The Congress was in session, but every man rose and cheered wildly. Cries of "Speech! speech!" rang on all sides of the densely packed chamber. I could not resist the call. I said:

"I am glad that the march of America's greatness has given liberty, after so many ages of injustice, to the most picturesque and romantic nationality in the world. You have preserved the very spirit of antiquity in the midst of all the commonplace bustle of modern life. But do not permit the element of conservatism, so strong in the race, to drag your new nation back into the thirteenth century. You must advance into the twentieth century, emulous rivals of all that is best and greatest in the age in which we live. The past has its honors, but the present has its duties. God made them both, and the present will be hereafter the past. No era in the world's history can approach our own in grandeur or importance. Ireland, the most composite nation of Europe, stocked from the best bloods of all races, since the time of the Atlanteans and the Phœnicians, filled with a fire that seems to come out of the very soil, must rise to the level of her great opportunities; and, by the thorough education and culture of all her people, present to the world the best intellects which can possibly arise out of her great stock. The nations have no nobler duty than this, for there is nothing higher on earth than the highest manifestations of the human mind. Let Ireland enter upon the tremendous future that awaits the world, with the solemn determination that Irishmen shall be inferior, in brain and character, to no people on earth."

The applause that followed this short speech was long-continued and deafening. At its close some one cried, "The Lady President!" and Sophie was forced, by thunderous cries, to come forward and speak. I can see, to this sad hour, the tall, lithe, emphatic, resolute figure, with the quick, instantaneous gestures, which added fire to the bright black eyes and strength to the incisive words. She said:

"Irishmen! I am glad to see you free and happy. May your wisdom, foresight and self-control keep you so forever. Passion is a great force in battle; but, in time of peace, we most need calm, discriminating reason. [Cheers.] The man who tries to excite you is not your friend. [Sensation.] Give up all old-time hates and love one another. I am glad to see Catholics and Protestants, the stern-faced northerner and the bright-faced southerner, Goth and Celt, all seated peacefully here, side by side, trying to make Ireland great and happy. [Immense applause.]

"Irishmen! Don't depress your women. [Cheers.] The barbarous races made women slaves; and something of the barbarian instinct survives in all civilized peoples. Remember that your men cannot be greater in soul than their mothers. [Applause.] Don't let sex be a disqualification, but give women a fair chance in every avenue of life. Macaulay called the Irish 'the Italians of the North of Europe,' and it was a profound observation. You have the genius as well as the ethnical affinities of that plastic and marvellous race, which once ruled the world, and produced the greatest men of antiquity.

"Irishmen! Remember this—that the man among you that permits his child to grow up in ignorance murders him! [Cheers.] Yes; he murders his soul, his mind, his opportunities, his happiness—his whole future. Look to it that you do not have to answer to God for that great crime. [Immense applause.]

"Farewell, and may God bless you."

The assemblage went wild; for Sophie, as I have remarked more than once, was always more popular than I. She seemed to have a way of getting right into the hearts of people. Is there another sense by which we are impressed with each other, apart from the slow operations of reason, sight, and hearing? Does soul talk to soul through flesh and bones; spirit reaching into the domicile of spirit; and the ghosts within us standing naked before each other? It may be.

Alas, as I draw nearer to the end of my story, I linger lovingly upon everything which concerns Sophie. I seem to see that bright vision forever before my eyes. It lives and breathes in the temple of my unhappy and distraught soul, a glorious yet dreadful memory. Poor—poor—dear—dear—Sophie! Why should such thing ever be and yet cease to be? O God! why dost Thou give to take away? And yet as one of our poets sings:

> 'Tis better to have loved and lost,
> Than never to have loved at all.

CHAPTER XLVII.

AMERICA.

NEVER did I know how much I loved America until I looked again upon its white strands.

And what a conception is that bronze figure, with the uplifted torch, welcoming the world; high, high up its trains its arm, as if it would reach and fire the very heavens.

Behind it should stand another figure; the peaceful, gentle, mother-figure, with the big, overflowing, dripping breasts, with which to feed the globe.

Liberty and abundance! The tremendous nation! What shall be named beside thee? A continent of food-fields, infused with the spirit of a merciful God! In thy great eyes I read the destiny of mankind; thou masterpiece of God's work on earth! Is there anything like unto thee among all the stars? Is this indeed the latest and perfectest work of the Almighty? Who shall say?

Long before we reached New York the harbor was thick with boats, skiffs, steamers, sailing vessels, black with people to welcome us home; and music, hurrahs, flags and banners filled the air.

But why dwell upon the series of ovations? How

little do all such honors seem to me now? I can remember dimly the mighty Broadway, lined with humanity from end to end; while, amid overwhelming uproar, a thousand zealous hands drew the chariot in which Sophie sat by my side, forgetting herself and proud solely of the honors paid to her husband. A true woman, who lived only in the man she loved; magnificent abnegation of the greater for the lesser; the divinity in human nature, ever sacrificing itself on the Calvary of its own heart for another and a less worthy.

My greatest joy was in witnessing the splendid prosperity of the people. It met us everywhere. There seemed to be no limit to the energy and triumph of humanity. There were no poor; every one was well dressed; none looked fatigued, none were sullen; every one smiled, all were happy.

The "Brotherhood of Justice" had done its work well while Sophie and I were absent; they had increased in number, so that the principal corporators now numbered over one hundred, all selected for their ability and love for mankind. In every direction their work had penetrated. They had greatly helped the cause of temperance, until the liquor-drinking habit had almost become a thing of the past. Through *The Anti-Monopolist* they were republishing all the greatest books of antiquity and of modern times. The humblest mechanic thus had upon his shelves, in the bound volumes of that paper, the best works of Greek and Roman authors, as well as of all the principal writers of the later nations. And this was not only true of literature, history, romance, but of all the recent acquisitions of science; the knowledge revealed by the telescope and microscope were brought home to millions of readers; and thus the whole population was rising to a mental status far above the most favored classes of a half-century ago. The lay members of the Brotherhood, male and female, had now reached to over twenty millions. In every state, county, and township there were organizations. State assemblies were held every year in groves, by lakes or rivers; the people bringing their tents, and living as cheaply as they could at home. In these gatherings everything was discussed that could advantage and benefit mankind; that was the sole object of all effort. Men worshipped God by helping their fellows. They believed with Coleridge,

> He prayeth best who loveth best
> All things both great and small;
> For the dear God who loveth us,
> He made and loveth all.

In every village, town and city there arose great labor-temples, and a myriad of lecturers were developed, who taught all the people all things that it was good for them to know; and nothing that would make men better or happier was too great or too small to be discussed, from the constitution of the solar system to the making of bread or the broiling of a beefsteak. And a splendid, wise, robust, handsome, learned, acute race was springing up; a kindly and generous race withal, and one whom no sophistry could deceive nor falsehood mislead; beyond comparison the most magnificent breed of men and women that had ever dwelt on the planet. And, in their splendid civilization, everything had its true place; they were neither sensualists nor ascetics; they ignored neither love nor duty; they enjoyed their earthly life, and never forgot the spiritual life in which they were embedded; and womanhood had its rights without becoming masculine, and men were strong without being brutal. And all the people were banded together by great associations. If one fell sick, his brethren cared for him; if he died his family were helped out of poverty by an insurance bounty. And if any man lacked strength or energy and tended to fall down into wretchedness or beggary, there were societies to put the hand of friendship under him, and make life easier, and at the same time self-respecting. And a strong sense of honor and dignity and duty to humanity spread everywhere; and an enlightened public opinion was the silent tribunal before which every one had to stand for judgment; for men could not be happy without the approval of their fellows. And it became evident that a few generations of men, thus living and acting, would vastly improve and elevate posterity; and that a new race would inhabit a new earth; and that all that was good in individuals to-day was but a type and figure of that which would be universal conditions in the near future.

Oh! It was a delight to move through and participate in such a world.

And so, witnessing all these tremendous results, which had flowed out of the Golden Bottle, I thanked the "Pity of God," who had brought it to me, and the inexpressible Divinity who, from beyond the stars, had taken pity on the estate of man, and had sent his messenger to me, in the days of my despair and wretchedness.

And so Sophie and I advanced, in one continuous uproar of salutation and adulation, from state to state and town to town, until we reached that marvellous city of. Chicago—the eighth wonder of the world, with a man's age and the wealth and power of an empire.

All day long we rode, or were drawn by the excited populace, through the streets of Chicago, swarming with rejoicing multitudes. At night we had a grand reception at our hotel, and all that was brilliant and eminent in the great city poured into the parlors to pay their respects to us.

At last, at twelve o'clock, completely tired out, after making our arrangements to proceed by special train on the morrow to Kansas City, Sophie and I retired for the night and were soon asleep.

CHAPTER XLVIII.

THE SOUND OF THE HAMMER.

It was the dim dawn of day when I awakened.

Dreamingly I looked up, with eyes half open, and began to count the knots in the rafters over my head.

It seemed very natural to find them there, for I had counted them a thousand times.

Gradually a sense of inconsistency broke in upon me. The rafters! Why, I was in the chamber of the Palmer House! There were no rafters visible here.

With a start I sat bolt upright.

Was I dreaming?

I was in the old garret at home!

How did I come there? Had I forgotten my journey from Chicago? I had intended to visit my former home and see my people, but it seems to me that I fell asleep last night in Chicago. I rubbed my eyes.

I put my hand into my breast. Sophie had made pockets in my undershirts, in which I carried my precious charge, the Golden Bottle. It was not there!

I got out of bed.

Where was Sophie?

I would dress myself. I must have come here yesterday, and through some freak of the over-worked mind, forgot all about the journey. Yes; that was it. And mother had put the President of the United States in his old garret, for a loving joke. Queer that I could not recall anything of it, however.

I looked for my broadcloth suit. There was nothing there but the ragged old clothes I had worn before my great rise in life. They were lying in a heap on the bare boards of the uncarpeted floor.

But the Golden Bottle? Had Sophie taken it? I did not relish such jokes. I would go downstairs and look after it. It was dangerous to have such a treasure passing from hand to hand. I had taken the utmost care of it for years and never before had it passed out of my possession. I felt very grave and somewhat indignant.

I drew on the ragged garments, with no little disgust; it was no way to treat a man in my position. Jokes are jokes, but there should be reason in all things.

Barefooted and bareheaded I passed down the creaking stairs. Strange; nothing seems changed, and yet father has been making improvements. He was too greedy to make money. These stairs should have been repaired. I will look after this.

I heard some one hammering on the outside of the house, near the front door, apparently driving tacks.

It was probably father. I stepped out. There was Bill Dickinson, that I used to know as a hanger-on about the court-house; he was tacking a paper against the side of the house.

"Hello, Ephe!" he cried familiarly, "just up?"

"What are you doing there?" I asked, with dignity.

"Puttin' up a notice of the mortgage foreclosure. Old Spooner thought it 'ud better be done to make sure."

"My God!" I gasped. "What does it all mean?"

Just then my mother appeared in the doorway. She looked very pale and haggard; she had been crying—her eyes were red; and her poor calico dress was torn, the colors had faded out of it years ago. She held a tin coffee-pot in her hand.

"Come in, Ephe," she said, "you look wild."

She had an idea I was about to assault the deputy sheriff.

I observed that the house was unpainted; there was no wind-mill—no garden fence. Where was father?

I followed mother into the house.

"Mother, mother, what does it all mean?" I cried.

"Ephraim, there is nothing but trouble. It is God's will; we must bear it."

I clutched my head with both hands. An idea— a terrible idea—had entered my mind.

"Mother," I said, "tell me one thing; when did I see you last?"

"My dear son," she said, putting her arms round

me and kissing me, "what is the matter with you? You look very strange; I hope you are not sick."

"Mother, tell me," I fairly shrieked, "when did I see you last?"

"See me last?" she replied with a bewildered look; "why, last night, of course."

"O my God!" I cried, "*then it was all a dream!*"

I fairly staggered; I tore my hair in agony; I glared wildly around me.

"Don't worry, my son," said my poor, frayed, poverty-stricken, weeping mother, "don't worry. Every one has his troubles. All the neighbors will have to go the same way. You remember the Hetheringtons who lived on the next farm. You remember Sophie."

"Yes, yes," I cried eagerly, "what of Sophie?"

"Why, the tin-peddler was along here at sun-up, and he told me that Sophie had gone to the bad, in Kansas City, and had hanged herself."

I whirled around as if I had been struck on the head with an axe, and fell prostrate on the floor.

CHAPTER XLIX.

MY LAST VISITOR.

FATHER, as I learned afterward, came in from the field; mother called him, and he and mother between them carried me back to the wretched straw bed in the garret, and laid me down upon it, and washed my face with cold water.

"O Sophie! Sophie!" were the first words I moaned as I recovered consciousness, "splendid, heroic, peerless Sophie!"

Father and mother exchanged glances.

Mother placed her hard hand, with all love and tenderness, on my burning forehead, and murmured:

"My poor boy! my poor boy! Bear up like a man."

"And the Golden Bottle!" I cried, clutching at my breast, and falling back helplessly.

My father, his face seamed with lines of care, placed his arm under my neck and kissed me, and mother sobbed and cried, "My poor boy! my poor boy!"

"O my God!" I moaned.

And then I struggled to rise—father holding me down—and shrieked:

"There is no God! That is a dream, too. If there was a God he never would have undone my work! O Sophie! Sophie!"

Father and mother drew apart from me and whispered. I could hear father speak the word "doctor," but mother shook her gray head sadly, and I caught the words "wouldn't come last time—pay."

"O my God!" I shrieked again; as the awful depths of our inexpressible poverty contrasted themselves with the splendor of the imaginations which still rose in panoramas in my memory.

Father and mother were both crying. Their looks told that they thought I had lost my mind—perhaps I had.

And then one noble thought rose like an angel in the midst of my miseries, and I said to myself:

"There is one thing that is not a dream—the love of these dear, tender hearts, who forget their own sorrows in my afflictions. That at least is godlike. I must not add new terrors to their distresses."

And so I spoke quite calmly.

"Dearest loves," I said, "do not worry about me. I am not crazy. I have had a tremendous dream, and it is hard to come back to the terrible reality. But I shall be better in a little while. Leave me to rest and think it over. I may forget my sorrows in sleep."

Mother wanted to get me some breakfast, but I could not have eaten a mouthful for the world; and so kissing me they withdrew, first drawing down the ragged paper curtain over the garret window, in which two panes of glass were broken.

When I heard the door close at the foot of the stairs, I sprang from the bed and fell on my knees and lifted up my long arms, with the worn sleeves and frayed wristbands, and while the tears rolled down my face, I prayed:

"O Omnipotent Power, whom men call God! Above all doubt and incomprehensibilities Thou must be. The universe could not be if Thou art not.

"O Father Supreme, if Thou didst not make this world as a cruel jest, have mercy on it.

"Thou seest its pitiful conditions! Thou seest the just impoverished and the wicked triumphant! Thou seest honesty profitless and crime profitable. Goodness grovels in the mud, while evil rolls in affluence.

"Across the ocean Thou seest three continents groaning under the weight of kings, courts, aristocracies and standing armies; and on this side another continent evolving these horrors out of the breast of liberty. Thou seest rotten and hollow hearts in the high places, and the humble overwhelmed with ignorance, superstition, and want. The lives Thou gavest to men are wasted, contending against adverse conditions; and millions die doubting and denying Thee. The minds of the few perceive what is needed to be done, but they are chained down by the thoughtlessness and selfishness of the multitude. The crust is small and hard in the mouth of the toiler, while he who toils not has a hundred times more than he can consume.

"From the inexpressible distance of Thy central throne, O Lord God Almighty, look down with mercy on this pitiful world, given over to the domination of ten thousand devils!

"Help the work of Thine own hands. Let the good thoughts that come from Thee be not dreams, but deeds. Lift up the people, O Lord! Wipe out injustice in all the world. Let Thy kingdom come on earth as it is in heaven. Help us, O Lord, help us! Let our prayers rise like screams of pain, and rouse Thee on the white throne of the central universe. Do not make us and forget us, O Lord God!"

I paused, for I heard a footstep behind me.

Now, what I am about to describe is something so strange that I doubted at the time my own sanity. Indeed, I had gone through so much—the troubles and sorrows growing out of the wretched condition of my family; the prolonged dream which had carried me through years of joy and glory; the horrible shock of awaking from a world redeemed to a world ruined; the sound of that hammer, tacking up the paper which was to sweep us from our home; and, above all, the horrible revulsion from the image of Sophie, the worshipped, the transcendent, the queen of the world, to the poor wretched girl dangling—O my God! I shudder as I think of it! All these things, I say, were enough to unsettle an intellect stronger than mine, for my whole system was enfeebled by disease.

The mind we carry about with us is an unknown world; no man can fathom its depths or possibilities of sound or unsound action. Indeed, it is impossible to say what is sanity and what is insanity. I was in an abnormal, unhealthy condition, that is certain; and the brain has power to create, within itself, as I had found, whole worlds of vivid phantasmagorias.

Hence, when I looked over my shoulder, without rising from my kneeling posture, I saw, walking up and down, in the garret behind me, the oddest figure I had ever beheld. It was that of an elderly gentleman, arrayed in the costume of the seventeenth century,—knee-breeches, cocked hat, gold buckles on shoes, sword by side, ruffled shirt, projecting, stiff collar and all. And a very energetic, snappy, prompt, active old gentleman he seemed to be. He had a short riding-whip in his hand, which every now and then he flicked impatiently.

I rose from my knees, and said, in a surly way, for I thought he was some wandering circus actor, who had found the doors open and climbed the stairs:

"Who the devil are you?"

He wheeled around and faced me, and, with a snap in his black eyes, and a snap in his voice, and a snap in his gesture, and a snap in his whip, he said:

"Devil yourself! I am what you are—a pinch of life in the dead wilderness—a fragment of the universal fire,—an instrument of the all-absorbing fate."

"What do you want here?"

"To tell you what a fool you are."

"Thank you," I said with something of my old presidential air, for I still believed he was human; "thank you, but do you think you have any right to intrude into a gentleman's bed-chamber, in that outlandish garb, and insult him?"

He glanced around the garret with a grin, and I could not help but smile myself, at the idea of calling it a "gentleman's bed-chamber."

"Tut, tut," he said, "don't be silly. I want to talk with you. It is two hundred years since I talked with a fool; and it reminds me of old times when I was a fool myself, and all the rest were fools with me."

"Two hundred years!" I cried, my hair beginning to stir.

"Certainly," he replied, "you don't suppose I could find such a suit of clothes as this in your beastly state of Kansas? I am a pictorial reproduction, on the retina of a human intellect, of something that lived and breathed and loved and sinned and died two hundred years ago in bonny, bosky England. Oh, the occult powers of nature! You couldn't find an identifiable particle of this body, or this sword, or this suit of clothes, with all your microscopes, in all the universe; the matter that made these ruffles is now a part of the nose of the Duchess Duras in Paris, and that which was this doublet now goes to make up the hide of a hyena, who at this moment is prowling after a caravan, not far from Damascus.

And yet, here am I, hat, wig, ruffles, knee-breeches, buckles, and all, and immensely tickled to be back on this foolish, silly old globe again, talking my native language to a long-legged boy of Yankee-land; although he does flatten out our broad, rich, guttural dialect into a nose-pinched, high-keyed, catarrhal mode of speech that is shocking. O Nature! Nature!" continued the garrulous old gentleman, "Nature is full of marvels; two hundred years ago this toggery, which I am parading in, impressed itself on my vital principle, and now my vital principle is able to impress it on yours; a photograph of a photograph; and a thousand years from now you may convey it, perchance, to some fellow in Mars. Nothing perishes that has ever had anything to do with a living spirit. The other day an old Phœnician pirate, who died five thousand years ago, daguerreotyped, on my receptivity, a picture of the sea-fight in which he was killed, just as he saw it, with his last look. It took place at the upper end of the Mediterranean. Oh, it was marvellously vivid! I could see the brown-faced wretches slashing and stabbing each other, in their long triremes; clinching and going overboard into the stained waters, glaring into each other's eyes in the most horrible manner. Ugh! it was awful. There isn't any other animal so desperately fierce and wicked as man."

"I have no doubt of it," I replied, "and at another time I should be delighted to have the privilege of listening to one of your vast experience, but I am plunged in unutterable miseries; and one whom I loved——"

"Pish!" he said contemptuously, "don't whimper. Sophie's all right. That tin-peddler was a liar—pardon my blunt speech;—we were a plain-spoken people two hundred years ago. You smell sweeter to-day, but you are not half as wholesome. We talked the coarseness we didn't act; you act the coarseness you don't talk. Now, as I said the other day to Socrates——"

I rushed toward him.

"For God's sake, tell me——"

An indescribable expression of terror came over the face of my visitor, and he fell upon his knees, clasped his hands and looked upward, with a wonderful awe upon every feature.

"Hush!" he whispered. "Don't name the Unnamable!"

"But if you are a spirit you must be near——"

He raised his hand and, with a look of pain on his face, stopped me.

"If this earth," he said solemnly, "was moved one hundred millions of miles nearer the Milky Way, are there any instruments known to man that would mark the decrease? No, no;" he continued, still on his knees, "it is true I am a spirit, but the world is full of spirits, cycles upon cycles of creators, universe enfolding universe of activities and labors, endless arrays of angels and archangels, cherubim and seraphim—but beyond all, within all, is THAT which we do not dare to name, and scarcely dare to think on."

He rose to his feet, but his snappy, pert manner was all gone.

"Pardon me," I said, "for using our common earthly blasphemy, born of ignorance and thoughtlessness, but you spoke of one who is very dear to me. You said——"

"Yes," he interrupted me, smiling again, "Sophie isn't dead, and she didn't go to the bad. She is a bright, high-spirited, energetic girl. She is working hard to support the body she is now in; she will make her way, and you will marry her some day, for she has a warm spot in her heart for you."

I rushed forward and seized his hand—there was nothing but air in my grasp. He smiled merrily and said:

"Mental, mental! You will never know until you 'shuffle off this mortal coil,' as my friend Sir Francis says, how much of all the phenomena of the world is mental and how much physical. There is no light where there are no eyes; no heat or cold where there is no sensation; and, to quote again from Sir Francis, 'nothing is but thinking makes it so.' Everything that seems to be is but the outcome of a great Force" (his face grew solemn again)—"phases of *His* thought. He falls into contemplation and universes rush into being. He smiles and the fathomless depths of space glow with light. The worship of all creatures above man is simply thinking; for to think is, with them, to adore."

"But," I said sadly, busy with my earth-affairs in the midst of his philosophy, "I can never marry Sophie—this consumption will——"

"Pshaw!" he said, with his first brusqueness, "consumption! You've got no consumption—simply throat trouble, born of sitting in the shade and sulking and slumping. 'Get a hump on yourself,' as you say in Kansas. If you don't the microbes will devour you. The lazy man is doomed. Nature has a million billion little devils to eat him up. If he won't work he is colonized by uncountable quantities of creatures that will work, and work him off the planet. Nature has no charity for sluggards. It is one, great, organized-energy; and no spirit has any right to the possession of a particle of matter unless he keeps it fully employed. Hence ten men rust out where one man wears out. Those who do most live longest. Hence the saying that the busiest man has always most time. Hence——"

I had to interrupt him or he would have run on forever, and my own affairs were pressing sorely on me.

"What am I to do?" I asked.

"Do?" he replied, "go to work."

"What at?" I inquired.

"*Write out your dream,*" he replied.

I staggered back.

"But men will laugh at anything so improbable."

"Not a bit of it," he said. "That dream is an allegory. The Golden Bottle represents the power of government to create its own money. With that power it will do all that you dreamed the Bottle did. It will make money so abundant that the credit system will cease, debts will disappear. You should have heard Aristotle and Sir Isaac Newton laughing, the other day, with old King Poseidon, of Atlantis, over the supreme folly of continuing the adoration of the sun and moon, through their metals, down into a Christian civilization of a high order. They fairly held their sides and shrieked; and old Poseidon said that men were nearly as incapable of new ideas as monkeys; and they laughed louder than ever; and thereupon Darwin introduced his theory of evolution, and they all grew melancholy and the conclave broke up. But don't you see," my visitor continued, "that the government by buying or constructing one railroad line—it owns a mortgage on one or two already—could put down rates and squeeze all the billions of water out of railroad stock, and leave $300,000,000 a year in the pockets of the people. Oh, the power of government, in other words of aggregate humanity, has not been one-tenth developed yet; and posterity will laugh at this generation. And your allegory is true in another respect. Within the next twenty-five years America will have to lift up Europe, by wiping out the kings and aristocracies, or go down to ruin under the feet of armed mobs, driven to desperation by wretchedness. The world has got to be—

wasn't it your great man, Abraham Lincoln, used the expression—'all free or all slave.' There is an irrepressible conflict that takes in the planet. You see, the government——"

Now I ought to have been intensely interested in all this; while I was President I would have been. But poor Ephe Benezet, in rags, was a different man from the conqueror of Europe. And how poverty ensmalls a man! A hungry man can think of nothing but food; a poor devil who is down can do nothing but struggle to get up. Large thoughts belong to large places. And so, while this wonderful being was talking of Aristotle and Poseidon, I was turning over in my head how I could get out of the slough of misery in which I found myself; and at length I interrupted him to ask the question.

"Do?" he said, with a snap, displeased at being brought down from great governmental questions to so small a thing as myself, "Do? Why, teach school. And then get to be a professor. A very ordinary school-teacher will make a first-class professor. There isn't one in a hundred that wouldn't rather hang himself than indulge in original thought; and nothing passes among them that has not the brand of some other professor. A schoolmaster is a teacher who is still capable of learning; a professor is a schoolmaster ossified. Their memories are magnificent—their reasoning faculties *nil*."

It was wonderful how he rambled off, flicking his whip, snapping his eyes, walking up and down and indulging in these heterodox and extravagant ideas.

"And Sophie," I said.

"Yes, Sophie; fine girl;" he replied, "I see her every day. She is descended from an English lassie I knew two hundred years ago—Lady Arabella Stanishurt—looks like her too; same eyes and way of carrying herself; same trick of the shoulders—pass for her daughter. Funny world, this. Nothing perishes. People crop out two hundred, five hundred years after they die. Men resemble ancestors they never heard of. I saw a carter the other day in London—lineal descendant of King Canute—had his very nose—nostrils looking out like eyes, straight ahead of him. That carter never heard of King Canute. And yet——"

"But," I interjected, "how did Sophie come to play so important a part in my dream?"

"All allegory," he replied; "Sophie represented the woman of the future: educated, intelligent, heroic, affectionate, refined; a million miles above the peasant woman in the mud; able to ride the savagest boor into obedience,—the sublimation of heart and brain combined."

"Now, one question more;" I said, "you heard my prayer——"

"Yes; and a very silly prayer it was," he interrupted. "You wanted a perfected world! What would you do in a perfected world? What would there be for any one to do—but lie on your backs and catch peaches in your mouths? Don't you know the universe is nothing but *work*, and we all of us—you and I, and the rest—have no place in it but as *workers*. Look back and see how mankind has advanced since man dwelt under a rock, and dined off the chap on the other side of the creek—cracking his head with a stone. Hasn't there been a tremendous amount of work done? Do you think the fellows who did all that are idle now? Not a bit of it, they are working harder than ever. And don't you think that you are expected to work just as hard as they did? Can't you see that every wrong that exists is simply an opportunity for genius and power to crush it? And do you suppose that there is no one looking after this big universe? Where did all this human unrest come from? Who stirred up all these countless leaders in every rural district, and every shop and mine, to forget sin and selfishness and devote themselves to the good of humanity? And if your family has been driven off the land by evil conditions, what is the remedy? To lie down and die? No; to get up and fight to the utmost limits of your last morsel of power. And do you imagine, you clay and lime and silex chaps, that this is your battle? No, it is a revolution of the spirits. Don't you know—or can't you conceive, (it seems plainer than that big nose on your face), that this is not a barren universe. It does not consist of the Un-named at one extremity and man at the other, with only vacuum between. No; every inch of space is packed with spirit, even as every inch of matter is packed with life; for life is only spirit with its clothes on. And, behind every man who labors to help the world, there are a thousand blessed spirits; and behind every bad man there are——"

Here he grew suddenly pale and stopped short, as if he had said too much.

"Tell me something about the hereafter," I said.

"There is no hereafter," he replied gruffly, "it is one eternal *is*. We create, you create, everything creates. The angels have made nothing more wonderful than some of the inventions of man. The birth of a flower is nothing to the evolution of the human mind under education. Compare the mechanism of one of your machines with the mechanism of an animal. What animal is more complicated or more perfect than one of your lightning printing-presses? And is not that press more necessary for the advancement of the world than a giraffe, with his long neck and inconsequential head—fitted only to browse the tops off trees? And do you think the spirit-world made one and did not make the other? No; this carpet of the illimitable creation is all of one pattern and all taken out of the same loom."

"Tell me," I asked, "what is to be the final outcome of man's civilization on earth? Will it end in a cosmical cataclysm?"

He was pacing rapidly up and down—in his testy way,—striking his knee-breeches, on the left side, smart taps with his whip; and as I asked this question he struck, as if impatiently, a smarter blow than usual. To my utter astonishment the whip passed completely through his thigh, and I saw it whirl round and round for an instant, through nothingness. He was gone!

I never was so astounded in my life.

I looked at the spot intently for a few minutes— then advanced and passed my hands through it. There was nothing there.

What did it all mean?

Had I really talked with an inhabitant of another sphere? Or were these my own thoughts, reflected back upon my mental consciousness? Was it all a dream,—like the Golden Bottle?

But I was greatly cheered, anyhow. I would write to Sophie. I would go to work. And I would tell my story to the world.

THE END.

The Works of . . . .
. . . . John Ruskin.

The D. D. Merrill Company has purchased from Messrs. John Wiley & Sons their Octavo, Twelvemo, and new Eighteenmo editions of Ruskin's Complete Works, and assures all students of Ruskin that neither expense nor pains shall be spared in maintaining the high reputation of the Wiley editions.

Descriptive Catalogue of all our publications sent on application.

D. D. MERRILL COMPANY,

**44 and 45 Bible House,
NEW YORK.**

ST. PAUL.

Some of JOHN RUSKIN'S CHOICEST BOOKS

IN ✢ HOLIDAY ✢ BINDING.

FORGET-ME-NOT EDITION.

The following are bound with white vellum cloth backs, embellished with a beautiful gold vine and forget-me-nots, Lansdowne silk sides, the daintiest conception of the year. Each, $1.50.

Sesame and Lilies.   Ethics of the Dust.
Crown of Wild Olive.   Queen of the Air.
Seven Lamps of Architecture. With 14 full-page plates.
Lectures on Architecture. With 15 full-page plates.
Stones of Venice. (Selections.)
Poetry of Architecture.
Val D'Arno. With 13 full-page plates.
Elements of Drawing.

Selections from Ruskin:
Frondes Agrestes. Readings from "Modern Painters."
True and Beautiful in Nature, Art, Etc. 2 Vols.
Precious Thoughts. Moral and Religious.
Pearls for Young Ladies.

Ruskin's Autobiography: Præterita. 3 Vols.

D. D. MERRILL COMPANY,
PUBLISHERS,
New York and St. Paul.

Story of an Emigrant

BY

Hon. HANS MATTSON.

Profusely Illustrated, Cloth, 8vo, $2.00.

This is a true story of an eventful life, and it can but have a healthful influence upon the life of every youth and young man who reads it. It is alike interesting to people of all ages and conditions in life. Were it not for the modesty of the author, it might justly be called "From a Poor Boy to a President." Note what a few have said:

General Johnson says: "My Dear Colonel:—I received my copy of your book on Saturday and read it through before retiring for the night. I expected a treat and was not disappointed. The trials of an emigrant are vividly set forth, and what you say about India gave me just the information I wanted. It is a splendid book and ought to have a large sale."

Jay Cooke, of Philadelphia, says: "I have read your book and have found it deeply interesting. You have paid but a just tribute to that noble class who have come over from the old country and have become so completely and creditably citizens of our great nation. I wish to distribute some of the books; send me 25 copies to begin with."

Hon. John G. Wicks, of Jamestown, N. Y., says: "It is a book that should be in every library of this liberty-loving country of ours, for it shows the possibilities for every one who is willing to work, is honest and ambitious. The reading of your book cannot fail to give courage to every one wishing to better his condition."

D. D. MERRILL COMPANY,

PUBLISHERS,

New York and St. Paul.

Tales of a Garrison Town,

BY

ARTHUR WENTWORTH EATON

AND

CRAVEN LANGSTROTH BETTS.

ILLUSTRATED BY

CHARLES HOWARD JOHNSON.

12mo.   cloth, $1.25.

An Entirely New and Unique Field of Fiction.

Short Stories of Great Range and remarkable Dramatic Power, portraying the military and social life of Halifax, Nova Scotia; with six full-page Pen and Ink Illustrations.

D. D. MERRILL COMPANY,

PUBLISHERS,

New York and St. Paul.

Glimpses of the Nation's Struggle

OFFICIAL PAPERS

READ BEFORE MINNESOTA COMMANDERY, LOYAL LEGION, FROM 1885 TO 1889.

THE FIRST VOLUMES ISSUED BY ANY COMMANDERY.

NO WAR LIBRARY IS COMPLETE WITHOUT THEM.

THE STORIES OF THE BOYS WHO FOUGHT NEVER LOSE INTEREST.

Two vols. Each, cloth, $2.00; half calf, $3.50.

D. D. MERRILL COMPANY,

PUBLISHERS,

New York and St. Paul.

www.ingramcontent.com/pod-product-compliance
Lightning Source LLC
Chambersburg PA
CBHW031901220426
43663CB00006B/724